Daniel Henry Haigh

The Anglo-Saxon Sagas

An Examination of their Value as Aids to History

Daniel Henry Haigh

The Anglo-Saxon Sagas
An Examination of their Value as Aids to History

ISBN/EAN: 9783744767613

Printed in Europe, USA, Canada, Australia, Japan

Cover: Foto ©Thomas Meinert / pixelio.de

More available books at **www.hansebooks.com**

THE ANGLO-SAXON SAGAS;

AN EXAMINATION OF THEIR VALUE AS AIDS TO HISTORY;

A SEQUEL TO THE "HISTORY OF THE CONQUEST OF BRITAIN BY THE SAXONS."

BY DANIEL H. HAIGH.

> " Hic reges populosque vides, quos alea fati
> " Extulit et pressit, sed ab his metire futura.
> " Aspice——quo devenere potentes:
> " Aspice quam uibili sit honor, lux, gloria mundi."
> HENRY OF HUNTINGDON.

LONDON:
JOHN RUSSELL SMITH,
36, SOHO SQUARE.
1861.

TO JOSEPH MAYER.

My dear Sir,

TRANGE as the theory which is advocated in the following pages may appear, it is advanced with an entire conviction of its truth. In part, —as far as it relates to the Scyldings and their settlements in Northumbria,—it has been already submitted to the Society of Antiquaries of Newcastle-on-Tyne, and an abstract from my papers, accompanied by illustrative notes from the pen of their able secretary, Mr. Longstaffe, has appeared in their Transactions. These notes are incorporated in the present work, together with other valuable information kindly furnished by him to me.

Under any circumstances, we have reason to be proud of these noble remains of the poetry of our forefathers; but our interest in them must be greatly increased, when we discover that they are based, not on mythological superstitions, but on historical facts; that they relate to a period, not of indefinite antiquity, but of the occupation of Britain by the Teutonic race; that they are not borrowed from any foreign source, but are entirely our own. With the hope, that you will find this little book, as a key to these sagas, worthy of your acceptance,

I remain, my dear Sir,

Very faithfully yours,

DANIEL H. HAIGH.

Erdington, July 27th, 1861.

CONTENTS.

CHAPTER I.

	Page
THE chronicled history of the fifth century is imperfect	1
The Anglo-Saxon sagas partly supply what is wanting	2
The poem of Beowulf. Opinions with regard to its origin, and subject-matter	ib.
Its internal evidence proves, that it was originally composed in Northumbria, about the middle of the sixth century	3
The Lament of Deor, the Traveller's Tale, and the Saga of Waldhere, also belong to England, and enable us to understand the later Teutonic sagas.	4
The latter appear to have been founded on traditions, which passed from England to the continent in the sixth century	5
A parallel to this theory in the circumstances of the Heliand.	6
In the Nibelungen series, old sagas have been designedly transformed into mere romances.	7
The historic value of Beowulf supported, in one instance, by Gregory of Tours.	8

CHAPTER II.

The story of Scyld Scefing	10
This story appropriated by Æthelweard, William of Malmsbury, and Simeon of Durham, to Sceaf, the head of the Anglo-Saxon genealogy	11
Scyld Scefing and Beowulf of the poem, have nothing to do with Sceaf, Sceldwa, and Beawa, of the genealogy	13
Beowulf, Healfdene, and his sons, a continuous descent	15

CONTENTS.

	Page
The story of Scyld, purely Anglo-Saxon	15
Scyld, Beowulf, and Healfdene, probably reigned in Northumbria	16
Heremod, (apparently a son of Healfdene), and Sigemund	18
Heorogar and Hrothgar	20
Hrothgar's residence, at Hart in Durham	ib.
Feud with the Beards	22
Grendel	23
The court of Hrothgar, at the time of Beowulf's visit	24
Later fortunes of this family	26

CHAPTER III.

The fight at Finnesham	29

CHAPTER IV.

Hrethel, king of the Geats, probably one of the associates of Hengest, resided for a time in Yorkshire, and then went to Suffolk	37
His children, Herebeald, Hætheyn and Hygelac	39
Hætheyn and Hygelac succeeded him. Their feud with Ongentheow and the Sweos	40
Hygelac's fall in battle with the Franks	45

CHAPTER V.

Wærmund, king of the West-Angles, reigned at Warwick	50
Two of his nobles endeavoured to set aside the succession of his son Offa, on the ground of physical incapacity, were defeated in council, appealed to arms, and perished in battle	51
The result of this battle was an extension of Wærmund's territory. Its scene identified on the borders of Gloucestershire and Oxfordshire	52, 53
Wærmund resigned the government in favour of Offa, died, and was buried at Gloucester	56
The story of Offa's queen	ib.

CHAPTER VI.

Three versions of the story of Horn	62
Heatholaf, his father, reigned in Yorkshire	63
His death	64
The fortunes of Horn	68

CHAPTER VII.

	Page
Beowulf adopted by Hrethel; his aquatic contest with Brecca	71
Accompanied Hygelac in his expedition against the Sweos	72
His voyage to Heort, conflict with Grendel, and return [1]	ib.
Was admitted by Hygelac to partnership in the kingdom	75
Took part in Hygelac's expedition against the Franks	76
Refused to take the kingdom into his own hand, to the prejudice of his cousin Heardred, after Hygelac's death	77
Became sole ruler of the Geats, after Heardred's death	78
At feud with the Wiwings	79
Called to reign over the Scyldings, after the fall of Hrothgar's race. The arrival of Eoppa and Ida	80
Ida's reign in Bernicia	81
Beowulf's adventure with a dragon; his death	82
The scene of this adventure identified	84
The death of Beowulf immediately preceded the accession of Ælle; he was probably of the same race	86
Wiglaf, the son of Weohstan	88
Wulf and Eofer, the sons of Wonred	89
Wlph, the adversary of Urien of Rheged	90
Connection of the heroes of the poem of Beowulf with the ancestors of five of the Anglo-Saxon royal dynasties	ib.
The succession of the first sovereigns of Deira and Bernicia	91

---

[1] (Note to page 75):—
I have said that the speed at which the cobles, used on the Yorkshire coast, can sail, with a fair wind, is about eight miles an hour. "Eight or nine," was the answer to a query on this head, addressed to a friend resident on the coast, who derived his information from the fishermen themselves; but a sailor, to whom I put the same, and who was less likely than the fishermen to give a favourable estimate of the sailing powers of their craft, said "seven;" and this I think is rather under the mark. However, since the note to page 75 was printed, I have met with something which I had previously overlooked, and which will enable us to form a more precise judgment as to the speed of Beowulf's vessel.

In the tenth century, the discoverer of America, Biorn Heriulfsson, favoured by a brisk S.W. wind, made the voyage from Newfoundland to Greenland in four days. The distance is 565 miles in a direct course, and this gives over 140 miles a day—about six miles an hour. Now a voyage of about 160 miles would bring Beowulf's vessel, after coasting Norfolk as far as Cromer, and then steering direct for Hart, within sight of Flamborough Head, the first high cliff on the Yorkshire coast. This, at six miles an hour, would require twenty-seven hours. The time stated in the poem seems to refer to the hour when Beowulf and his companions first saw land; and from this point they would be able to prosecute their voyage, and reach the court of Hrothgar in the evening (for the evening meal immediately followed their arrival).

APPENDIX.

	Page
Remarks by Mr. Howitt, Mrs. Jameson, Mr. Walbran, and Mr. Longstaffe, on dragon-stories generally	95
Series of these stories from the tenth to the fifteenth century .	97

CHAPTER VIII.

The Lament of Deor. Weland and Beadohild	101
Geat and Mæthhild	103
Theodric and Eormanric. Deor and Heorrenda . . .	104
The Traveller's Tale	105
The time of the Traveller's journey	106
All the princes he names, except Alexandreas, were of Barbaric race	ib.
He certainly travelled in this island	107
Traces remain, in this country, of the presence of most of the tribes whom he visited	108
In some instances these are accompanied by other traces, of the princes whom he mentions as ruling these tribes . . .	114
Other traces again, of princes whom he visited . . .	118
His Eormanric was the father of Æthelberht, king of Kent . .	121
His Ætla, a king of Huns, who reigned, first in Warwickshire, and afterwards in Norfolk	122
His Gifica, Guthhere, and Gislhere, kings of a part of the Burgundian nation, who were settled in England . . .	124
The fragments, lately discovered, of Waldhere's saga . . .	125
Gerald of Fleury's Latin version of the same . . .	128
The story of Eormanric and Theodric, as collected from the sagas	131
Traces of the connections of Eormanric, in the districts of which Oxford is the centre	133
The story of Ætla	138
Traces of his connections in Warwickshire and Leicestershire, and in Norfolk	139
The Burgundian princes	140
Their course traced from Middlesex, through Essex, to Ætla's kingdom	141
Irminfrid of Thuringia; his war with Theoderic, king of the Franks	142
Hadugot, the ally of Theoderic	143
Irminfrid's flight to Ætla	144
His death	145

	Page
The Traveller's journey was made early in the reign of Eormanric, and of Theoderic the Frank	146
His home was in Cheshire or North Staffordshire; he traversed the midland districts, and spent some time in the territories of Eormanric	147
Deor lived within the territories of Eormanric, but after his death	148
The Traveller was probably Hama	ib.
The Lay of Hildibrand	149

CHAPTER IX.

Cyneric, king of the West Saxons. Death of Wihtgar. Ida, king of Bernicia. The battle of Salisbury	156
The battles of Barbury and Hardenhuish	157
Ælle, king of Deira. Dutigirn, the antagonist of Ida. Maelgwn, king of Gwynedd	158
Urien of Rheged, and other British princes; their conflicts with the Angles; Wlph and Flamdwyn	159
Adda, king of Bernicia; Ceawlin, king of the West Saxons; Æthelberht, king of Kent	160
Clappa and Theodwulf, kings of Bernicia; the battles of Wembdon and Bedford	161
Frithuwulf, king of Bernicia; the battle of Derham . . .	162
Theodric, king of Bernicia; the battle of Arderydd . . .	163
The siege of Medcaut (Lindisfarne); death of Urien . .	164
The battles of Mondrum and Fadley	167
Æthelric, king of Bernicia; the battle of Cattraeth; Æthelric and Frithuwald, kings of Deira; the battle of Wanborough .	168
Æthelfrith, king of Bernicia; the arrival of S. Augustine; Ceolric and Ceolwulf, kings of the West Saxons . . .	170
Hussa, king of Deira; the battle of Dalston	171
Æthelfrith's conquest of Deira; the family of Ælle . .	173
Cynegils and Cwichelm, kings of the West Saxons; the battle of Bampton	174
The battle of Chester	175
British tradition relative to the early years of Eadwine, the son of Ælle	177
His accession to the throne of the united kingdoms of Deira and Bernicia. Conclusion	178

THE ANGLO-SAXON SAGAS.

CHAPTER I.

Their Historic Value.

HE system of chronology, which has been maintained in the "History of the Con-"quest of Britain," enables us to recognize a groundwork of historic truth, in stories which have hitherto been regarded as mere romances. To have discussed, in that work, such of these stories as belong to the fifth century, would not only have broken the chain of our history, but would have been premature, whilst the chronology itself was in question; but now that we have established our system as a framework wherein to place them, we are in a position to enter upon this, the most interesting department of our inquiry.

The history of the fifth century, although it presents us with an unbroken chain of events, is necessarily imperfect with regard to the gradual establishment of the Saxon kingdoms, because its notices of the Saxons are most entirely

confined to those who came into conflict with the Britons.
The kings of Kent appear at intervals until A.D. 487; the
kingdom, founded in Northumbria by Octa, ceases with the
fall of Colgrim in A.D. 471; a kingdom rises in Sussex,
holds for a time the supremacy over the other Saxons in
Britain, and yields it in A.D. 498 to Wessex. The ancestors of the Bernician, Deiran, East Anglian, Mercian, and
East Saxon dynasties, accompanied or followed Horsa and
Hencgest to Britain, and probably founded principalities;
but the history says nothing about them or their children,
because they either were not engaged in the wars of their
time, or, if they were, appeared only as followers of Octa,
Colgrim, Ælle, or Garmund.

To the Cambrian genealogist we are indebted for the facts,
that Seomel was the first, of the ancestry of Ælle of Deira,
who conquered that province and Bernicia, and that Wiwa
was the first of his line, who reigned in Britain over the East
Angles; and the existing remains of the epic poetry of our
forefathers, whilst they relate chiefly to events of the sixth
century, tell us something of the second Hencgest, of Offa,
of Seomel's son Swerting, and of others who reigned in
Britain during the fifth century, whilst the great conflict was
going on, and before the establishment of the kingdoms, which
figure in the history of a later time.

Of these remains the poem of Beowulf is the grandest; it
has deservedly engaged the attention of the most eminent
scholars of Germany, Sweden, and Denmark, as well as of
our own country; but unfortunately it has been very much
misunderstood. Its origin has been referred to the Scandinavian kingdoms, and to a period antecedent to the immigration into Britain of the Teutonic race; and its subject to the

misty regions of mythology. One eminent scholar, Mr. Thorpe, has expressed his conviction that the heroes of this poem are real kings and princes of the North, whilst he assigns to them a home in Sweden.[1] I claim for it an English origin, and, (although in a different sense from that in which he puts them), adopt his queries, and the answer to them:—

"What interest could an Anglo-Saxon feel in the valorous "feats of his deadly foes the Northmen? in the encounter of "a Sweo-Gothic hero with a monster in Denmark? or with "a fire-drake in his own country? The answer, I think, is "obvious—*none whatever.*"

And, I think, the same answer must be given to the query, "What interest could an Anglo-Saxon feel in translating "such a poem for his countrymen?"

I regard it as the composition of a Northumbrian scóp, familiar with the scenes he describes, and acquainted with persons who had been cotemporary with some of his heroes; I believe that all the events he records,[2] with two exceptions, occurred in this island, and most of them in Northumbria, during the fifth and sixth centuries.

In its present form, the poem is not older than the tenth century, but it bears the marks of having been transcribed from a much older original, in the retention of many forms of words, which we may regard as early Northumbrian, from their correspondence with those with which the Northumbrian

---

[1] He considers it a "metrical paraphrase of an heroic saga composed "in the south-west of Sweden, in the old common language of the North, "and probably brought to this country during the sway of the Danish "dynasty." Preface to Beowulf, VIII.

[2] Not including, of course, the giant and dragon stories.

monuments and the Durham Ritual have made us acquainted; and thus we obtain the first indication of the author's fatherland. His fidelity in descriptions of scenes, which we can identify beyond all doubt, even after the lapse of thirteen hundred years, supplies the second. A curious passage, in which he quotes the authority of persons who had been her cotemporaries, for the character of a certain princess, in such a way as to warrant the inference that he had conversed with them, shows that he must have composed his saga not very long after the events of which it treats. On the other hand, there is no allusion whatever to events later than the time of Ælle's accession to the throne of Deira; and with the exception of a few passages, which may have been added after the conversion of Northumbria to Christianity, and some allowance for embellishments, we may believe that it comes to us in substance as it was originally delivered by its author.

The Lament of Deor, the Traveller's Tale, and the recently discovered fragments of a saga of Waldhere, are invaluable relics of the same class of literature. For these also I claim an English origin, and with their aid I shall be enabled to show, that Eormenric, Theodric, Ætla, and others who figure in the grand cycle of Teutonic romance, were kings and chieftains who flourished in England, in the first half of the sixth century. Identified with Hermanaric and Theodoric, kings of the Ostrogoths, and with Attila, king of the Huns, their story presents the grossest anachronisms; the process is inconceivable, by which the great Attila of history could be cotemporized with Hermanaric, who died about a quarter of a century before he was born, with Theodoric, who was born two years after he died, and with Irminfrid of

Thuringia, who survived Theodoric some years; identified, on the other hand, with Eormenric of Kent, the cotemporary of Irminfrid, with Theodoric his nephew, and with an Ætla who certainly reigned in Norfolk, all these anachronisms disappear; and, however great may be the corruptions which have crept into the story which the cycle presents to us,—a story so popular that it was reproduced and embellished from age to age, for several centuries, and in different countries,— whatever details of the true history of Hermanaric, Theodoric, and Attila, may eventually have been incorporated with it, these sagas enable us to accept it as founded on fact, as substantially true.

In its earliest form we find it in an English dress, and it is easy to account for its appearance on the continent at a later time. The epoch, in which these heroes flourished, was also one of a great emigration to the continent; the conquest of Britain was complete, and large bodies of the Anglo-Saxons, by feuds and other causes, were forced to seek settlements abroad. They carried with them, of course, the traditions of their island home, and songs originally composed in England, recounting the exploits of their heroes, were sung at their feasts in France[3] and Thuringia. Traditions of the events which were connected with their expatriation, would be preserved from generation to generation; and these would be the groundwork of the German romances, which are all of comparatively modern date, abound in names of places and countries, bring together their heroes from all parts of Europe, and contain anachronisms even more startling than those

---

[3] When, for instance, the Hocings from Kent settled at Hocquinghem, they would not forget their hero Hnæf.

above noticed. One fragment alone of these songs remains in something like its original form,—the Lay of Hildebrand; it is referred with great probability to the eighth century, and almost equals Beowulf in its simplicity.

The theory that sagas, originally English, were carried to the continent, and formed the basis of a very popular cycle of romances, will be found to be borne out by facts which will be adduced in the following pages, and has its exact parallel in the circumstances of the Heliand. We know that the poetical works of our Cædmon[4] embraced the whole series of Scripture history, yet only a part thereof, relating the principal events of Genesis and Exodus, and a fragment treating of one of the events of the Captivity in Babylon, remain to us. The Heliand contains the Gospel story; and not only is it perfectly Cædmonian in its style, but there is a tradition which evidently relates to it, that in the reign of Louis the Pious, a herdsman received poetical inspiration in his slumbers, and on awaking turned the whole Scripture narrative, of the Old and New Testament, into excellent verse. Here is undeniably Bæda's story of Cædmon, localised in Germany; and it is very probable that the Heliand is one of the volumes of Cædmon's paraphrase, carried to Germany by an Anglo-Saxon missionary, and translated into the old Saxon dialect. So the sagas of Theodric and Ætla, of which we possess a fragment

---

[4] Sir F. Palgrave, Archæologia, xxiv. 342, has called in question the story, and the name of Cædmon. With regard to the story, we must remark that the subject of it must have been living in Bæda's childhood, in a monastery which had intimate relations with his own; and with regard to the name, that it has remained amongst us to this day (Cadman), and that in each of its elements it has its correspondents in other Anglo-Saxon names, Cædwealh, Cædbæd, Tilmon, Tytmon.

in their earliest form, and to which we have references in Beowulf, the Lament of Deor, and the Traveller's Tale, were conveyed by their cotemporaries to the continent, were translated into other dialects, as in the Lay of Hildebrand, and in later times amplified and corrupted, as in the Wilkina Saga and the Nibelungen Lied.

The embellishments of the stories in the Edda and Wilkina Saga are such as may have been made in good faith, by scalds whose object was to combine separate traditions, and to illustrate their subject with matter derived from other sources; but in the poems of the Nibelungen series, the old sagas, on which they are founded, have been designedly transformed into mere romances. This we learn from the poems themselves, and M. Thierry[5] has clearly explained the object with which this was done.

When the Emperor Otho the Great, at the battle of Augsburg, A.D. 955, conquered the Hungarians, he granted them peace, on condition of their receiving amongst them missionaries of the Christian faith. Pilegrin, one of the most eminent ecclesiastics of his time, superintended the Hungarian mission, and was made Bishop of Passau in A.D. 971. Sarolt, a sort of Amazon, a fit representative of Brunhild and Chrimhild, who rode, fought, and drank like a warrior, received the faith, and was the means of the conversion of her husband Geiza, who became chief of the Hungarian nation in A.D. 972, and was baptized in the following year. Under their auspices, the Hungarians became Christians, and although they apostatized some years later, and drove Pilegrin from his diocese, he had the consolation before his death, in A.D.

---

[5] Attila et ses successeurs, II. 349.

991, of seeing S. Stephen, the son of Geiza and Sarolt, seated on the Hungarian throne.

The Lament of the Nibelungen tells us that this Pilegrin wrote the story of Attila in Latin, and actually presents him to us as a cotemporary of Attila, receiving at Passau the news of the slaughter of the Nibelungen, resolving to put it on record, and engaging one of Attila's bards to assist him. The Nibelungen Lied introduces him in his palace at Passau, entertaining his niece Chrimhild on her way to Attila's court, and speaks of Attila's court as the centre of the propagation of the Christian faith, of a Christian church at Etzelburg, and of the baptism of Ortlieb, the son of Attila and Chrimhild. It is evident that the good bishop had in view the work in which he was himself engaged; his Attila, Chrimhild, and Ortlieb are no others than Geiza, Sarolt, and S. Stephen; the character of Attila, as he presents it, is that which he proposed for an example to Geiza; and ancient historic sagas have become a mere romance in his hands. We fortunately possess them, although but in a fragmentary condition, in their purest, their original form.

The exact accordance between the poem of Beowulf, and Gregory of Tours' History of the Franks, with regard to the circumstances of Hygelac's last expedition and death; and the general correspondence between this poem, the Traveller's Tale, and the S. Albans' tradition, with regard to the history and character of Offa; warrant us in considering these poems as historic, (every allowance, of course, being made, in the marvellous stories of Sigemund's and Beowulf's adventures with dragons, for the genius of a people who were disposed to regard everything extraordinary as supernatural). These and other marvels we put out of the question; they may or may not be later embellishments; our object will be, to endeavour to ascertain how much of the poem relates to the history of our country in the fifth and sixth centuries; the notices it contains of Hrothgar's family, of Hencgest, of Heatholaf and Horn, of Hygelac, of Beowulf, and of Offa, will be the subjects of the following chapters; and we shall then examine the Lament of Deor, and the Traveller's Tale, before we resume the history of the establishment of the Anglo-Saxon kingdoms.

CHAPTER II.

The Ancestors and Family of Hrothgar.

THE poem of Beowulf commences with the story of Scyld Scefing.

"Lo! We have heard of the Gar-Danes
" in days of yore, the power of mighty kings,
" how the æthelings achieved valour. Oft did Scyld Scef-
" ing tear away the mead-settles from the hosts of his foes,
" from many tribes; the warrior dismayed them, after he
" was first found destitute. Therefore he abode in com-
" fort, waxed under the welkin, throve in dignities, until
" every one of those sitting around, over the whale path,
" should obey him, pay him tribute. That was a good king.
" A son was afterwards born to him, young in the courts,
" whom God sent for comfort to the people. He knew the

---

[1] Following Mr. Kemble's prose translation for the most part, I have occasionally made use of Mr. Thorpe's, in the following series of quotations. The references are to the pages of the original MS., given in the margin of Mr. Kemble's edition of the text. I think it unnecessary to swell the bulk of this volume by citations of the text, as the poem is easily accessible, through the labours of these eminent scholars, and others on the continent.

"evil need they had suffered a long while, princeless. There-
"fore the Lord of life, the ruler of glory, gave him worldly
"honour. Beowulf, Scyld's son, was famous, his glory
"sprang widely in the divided lands."[2]

"Then, at the appointed time, Scyld, very decrepid, be-
"took him to go into the Lord's enclosure. His dear com-
"rades then bare him out, to the shore of the sea, as he
"himself, the friend of the Scyldings, the dear land chief,
"bade them, whilst he ruled his words; long he held it.
"The ringed ship, the ætheling's vehicle, icy and outward-
"bound, stood then at the hithe. Then they laid down the
"dear prince, the giver of rings, in the bosom of the ship,
"the great one by the mast. There were many treasures
"of ornaments, brought from far-ways. I have not heard
"of comelier keel, decked with war-weapons and battle-
"weeds, bills and byrnies. Many treasures lay on his bosom,
"that should depart with him far into the possession of the
"flood. They furnished him with offerings, princely trea-
"sures, not less than they had done, who sent him forth at
"the beginning, when a child, alone over the waves. More-
"over they set for him, high over head, a golden sign. They
"let the sea bear him, gave him to ocean. Sad was their
"spirit, mourning their mood. Men, hall-counsellors, heroes
"under heavens, knew not to say forsooth who received that
"freight."[3]

The tradition, of Scyld's exposure when a child, was known to some of our mediæval chroniclers, Æthelweard, William of Malmsbury, and Simeon of Durham; but they have erroneously connected it with Sceaf, the head of the Anglo-Saxon genealogy. I say erroneously, for I cannot but re-

---

[2] F. 129.   [3] F. 129, 130.

gard as a purer form of the legend, that which this poem presents to us; since its author must have lived some centuries nearer to the times of which he speaks, than Æthelweard, and tells us more of the history of this Scyld, than, (as far at least as appears), these later writers knew. His authority appears to be supported by other circumstances.

Æthelweard says,[4] that Scef, an infant, was found by the inhabitants of the isle of Scani, in a boat, which had drifted to their shore, laden with armour; that they adopted and educated him, and eventually elected him their king.

This tradition is evidently what is alluded to in the passage above cited; the only variation is in the name; and this is easily accounted for by the supposition, that Æthelweard, (or the authority whence he derived it), mistook Scefing for Sceaf, and attributed it to the only Sceaf of whom he had any knowledge, the head of the Anglo-Saxon genealogy. Having done this, he omits the whole series of generations between Sceaf and Sceldwa.

About a century and a-half later, William of Malmsbury[5] gives us another version, in which the circumstance of the armour is omitted, but another is introduced,—that of a sheaf of corn placed at the head of the child,—which can only be regarded as an addition to the story, suggested by the sup-

---

[4] "Ipse Scef cum uno dromone advectus est in insula Oceani, quæ dicitur Scani, armis circumdatus, eratque valde recens puer, et ab incolis illius terræ ignotus; attamen ab eis suscipitur, et ut familiarem diligenti animo eum custodierunt, et post in regem eligunt."

[5] "Iste Sceaf, ut ferunt, in quandam insulam Germaniæ Scandzam appulsus, navi sine remige puerulus, posito ad caput frumenti manipulo, dormiens, ideoque Sceaf nuncupatus, ab hominibus regionis illius pro miraculo exceptus, et sedulo nutritus; adulta ætate regnavit in oppido, quod tunc Slaswic nunc vero Haithebi appellatur."

posed meaning of the name. In the genealogy which accompanies it, he inserts the name of Sceaf between those of Heremod and Sceldwa. This shows that he was borrowing from sources independent of the genealogy, at the head of which he places Streph, saying of him, (what the Saxon Chronicle relates of Sceaf), that he was the son of Noe, born in the ark.

The truth is, that Scyld Scefing and Beowulf of this poem have nothing to do with Sceaf, Sceldwa, and Beawa of the genealogy. Misled by the similarity of the names, Æthelweard has attempted to identify them, and consequently has cut off from the genealogy the ancestry of Sceldwa; and William of Malmsbury, foisting Sceaf into a place which does not belong to him, has invented another name to take that which really does.

What has been stated in the " History of the Conquest of " Britain" with regard to Geat and Woden, applies equally to Sceaf, and the rest of his descendants; the names in the genealogy are the names of men, borne, not by these alone, but by others.

Sceaf is one of those names which seem to have descended from age to age, from the earliest post-diluvian times. Shebas are mentioned amongst the posterity of Ham and Shem; the Traveller speaks of a Sceafa as king of the Longobards; and we have found several traces in this country, either of this individual, or of a namesake. Heremod is a name of great antiquity. It is ascribed in the Scandinavian mythology to a son of the first Woden; it was borne, in the sixth century before the Christian æra, by the Athenian citizen, who delivered his country from the yoke of tyrants, (in honour of whom it was decreed that it should be given to no other);

it was also the name of one of the personages who are celebrated in this poem, and of others. The Scandinavian genealogy has not only Skiöld, corresponding to our Sceldwa, but a second, one of the sons of Woden, and the first king of Hleidre; and another, king of Varna, is mentioned in the Ynglinga Saga, cotemporary with Eystein king of Upsal; all perhaps, as well as the Scyld of our poem, namesakes of an original Scyld, of whom the statement[6] might be true, that he was the first colonist of Germany. Beowa occurs as the name of a witness to a charter[7] of Nunna, king of the South Saxons; and, as that of an earlier chieftain, one of the first colonists of Britain, in several local names.[8] Tætwa was the name of one of the kings of the Longobards.[9] Beowulf, a name which has never occurred but in this poem (in which two persons in no way related bear it), is certainly distinct from Beowa; but even were it the same, (as other instances show that the same person might have a short as well as a long name), the coincidence of Sceldwa and Beowa in the genealogy, with Scyld and Beowulf in the poem, would not be more remarkable, than that of the two cotemporary Eadberhts in the eighth century, each the son of an Eata.

I see no reason then for identifying Scyld and Beowulf with Sceldwa and Beowa, the ancestors of Woden, nor for supposing that the poet has omitted a long succession between Beowulf and Healfdene; on the contrary, I am convinced that they are distinct persons, who lived at different

---

[6] In a MS. at the Bibliothèque Impériale, 6055.
[7] Cod. Diplom. 1001.   [8] Beowanham, C. D. 353, for example.
[9] So also, when, lower in the genealogies, we find the names of Ossa, Eoppa, Ingwi, Offa and others, occurring in different lines of descent, we may well believe, that those who bore them were so named after heroes of earlier times, well remembered then, though now forgotten.

epochs. The poet clearly speaks of Healfdene as the son of Beowulf, in the same sense as Beowulf was the son of Scyld.

"Then was in the towns, a long time, Beowulf of the "Scyldings, the dear king of the people, famous among na-"tions; (his father had passed away, the prince from his "dwelling); until from him in turn sprang high Healf-"dene."[10]

And he uses precisely the same expression, immediately afterwards, in speaking of Healfdene's offspring:—

"Four sons, chiefs of hosts, numbered forth to him, sprang "into the world, Heorogar and Heothgar, and good Halga."[11]

It is clear that he speaks of a continuous succession, Scyld, Beowulf, Healfdene, Heorogar and his brothers.

The story of Scyld and the boat is purely Anglo-Saxon. The Danes knew nothing of it; their second Skiöld was the son of Woden, and received the kingdom from his father; and he was the first, according to their tradition, who bore amongst them the title of king. Yet if Woden came to Denmark at the time we have supposed, his son Skiöld may well have been living during the infancy of our Scyld, and his name have been bestowed by the people of Skäne on the child so mysteriously drifted to their shores, with the addition of the distinctive name *Scefing*, *i. e.* "the son of the "boat."[12]

---

[10] F. 130.

[11] There is a defect in the MS., and the fourth son of Healfdene is not mentioned here.

[12] For although our glossaries do not give *scef* as a name for a boat, the modern *skiff* proves that they had such a word, equivalent to the O.H.G. *scef*, Welsh *ysgaff*, Breton *scâff*, Erse *sgaffa*, Gr. σκάφη; and the word *sceofel, shavell* (Tusser), "shovel," indicates the existence of a verb *sceafan, sceof, sceafen*, from which it was derived, as σκάφη from σκάπτειν.

A writer in the Gent. Mag. 1857, August, p. 122, in reference to Wil-

This, I believe, is really the meaning of the word *Scefing*; and this meaning, understood no doubt when the Saxon Chronicle was compiled, may have suggested the idea that Sceaf, the head of the genealogy, was born in the ark. A child found under such circumstances would have, of course, no known father, no pedigree; it would therefore be quite natural to give him such a name as this, *Scefing* " the son of " the boat."[13]

That Scyld, Beowulf, and Healfdene reigned in Northum-

---

liam of Malmsbury's suggestion as to the derivation of this name, says " it is just as likely that he was named from the *schiff* or *skiff* in which " he came." *Schiff*, however, does not represent our *skiff*, but our *ship*.

[13] I suspect we have another notice of him, under another name. In the Anglo-Saxon rune-poem, the following stanza occurs :—

Ing wæs ærest,	Ing was first,
mid East-Denum,	among the East-Danes,
gesewen Secgum,	seen by the Secgas,
oth he siththan ést	until he after eastward
ofer wǽg gewát.	over the wave departed.
Wæn æfter ran.	Thought followed him.
Thus Heardingas	So the Heardings
them hæle nemdun.	named the hero.

Wæn in the sixth line, of course, is " waggon," but I do not see how this would make sense. I venture to read wén, and take it to mean that the regrets of his people followed him. The East Danes were subjects of Hrothgar, and Sigeferth, prince of the Secgas, appears, from the " Fight at Finnesham," to have been a vassal of Healfdene. The circumstances of Ing's mysterious appearance amongst these people, and his final departure over the sea, corresponding with Scyld's story, seem to indicate that he is the same person ; and the concluding lines accord with the supposition that he was known by another name. Besides, the poem of Beowulf supplies two circumstances confirmatory of this theory, that Scyld-Scefing and Ing were one ; the first, that Hrothgar's people, the Scyldings, are twice called Ingwinas ; the second, that Hrothgar gave Beowulf a sword, which had belonged to his brother Heorogar, and probably was an heir-loom in his family, and that Beowulf, in his last conflict, had a sword which had belonged to Incg.

bria, as Hrothgar certainly did, is very probable. Reckoning the generations upward from Hrothgar, we find that Scyld must have been living at the time, A. D. 375, when, as we have seen, an immigration of Saxons took place; and, at the beginning of the fifth century, the Secgas, subjects of this family, had given name to Segedunum, (*Secga-dún*), which became one of the stations of the wall. This, the most easterly station, was possibly the place which Simeon of Durham calls " Scythles-cestre by the wall," and Roger of Howden " Scylte-cestre;" a name which appears to contain that of Scyld, as those of the neighbouring North and South Shields do to this day. North of the wall, again, we have, in close proximity, Shilbottle, (*Scyldes-botl*), "the palace of Scyld," and Bolton on the Alne, and Boulmer, which may derive their names from that of Beowulf; the former, indeed, seems to be the Bolvelaunio of Ravennas, and to contain the names of Beowulf and Alauna, (*Beowulfi-Alaunium*), as it is placed next to Alauna, which is probably Alnwick.[14]

From these facts, I infer the probability, that Scyld, Beowulf, and the Secgas, had effected settlements on the coast of Northumberland, towards the close of the fourth century; and they might be the people who were received by Vortigern.

After the notice of the three sons of Healfdene, there is evidently a defect in the MS., so that the name of the fourth is lost. From the context it appears, that they were all sons, " heads of hosts;" and two passages, which will be cited immediately, make it almost certain that the fourth was Here-

---

[14] It may be the name of the river Alne, for although the list in which it occurs is professedly one of cities, the occurrence of Tamese among them shows that some of them may be rivers.

mod. Already established in Britain when Horsa and Henegest came, Healfdene and his sons would naturally make common cause with them, (besides being already in Vortigern's interest, if the original settlement of the family was made under his auspices). Accordingly we have found[15] traces of all their names, in districts marked by the presence of those chieftains.

On account of some feud, of which the origin is unknown, the subjects of Healfdene appear[16] to have been leagued with Henegest II. against Fin, the son of Folcwalda; and the following passages contain notices of other feuds.

"Heremod was not an honour to the children of Ecgwela,
"the Scyldings. He waxed not according to their pleasure,
"but for destruction, and for a deadly plague to the people
"of the Danes. Angry of mood, he destroyed his table-
"enjoyers, his near friends; until that he, the great prince,
"alone departed from the joys of men. Though the mighty
"God had exalted him with the joys of power, with energies,
"had advanced him above all men, yet there grew in his
"spirit a blood-thirsty disposition; he gave not rings to the
"Danes after judgment. He dwelt joyless, so that he en-
"dured the labour of war, a tedious public plague."[17]

Ecgwela was probably a prince of the Danes, before the days of Scyld; but there seems to be no other way of accounting for Heremod, than the supposition that he was the son of Healfdene. The next passage seems to represent him as an ally of Sigemund.

"Well he told everything that he had heard of Sigemund,
"of his valiant deeds, the battles, wide journeys of the Wæl-

---

[15] History of the Conquest of Britain, p. 159.
[16] See the following Chapter. [17] F. 167.

"sing, much unknown. Of those things, his warfare and
"crimes, the children of men knew not well, save Fitela
"with him. Then he would say something of this sort,
"how the uncle and his nephew were always sharers of hard-
"ship, in every conflict. They had cut down with their
"swords many of the race of the Eotens. No little glory
"sprang to Sigemund after his death-day, after the bold in
"war quelled the worm, the keeper of the hoard. He, the
"ætheling's son, alone ventured on the bold deed under a
"hoar-stone, nor was Fitela with him. Yet it chanced him,
"that his sword pierced through the wondrous worm, so that
"the noble iron stood fast in the wall; the dragon perished
"in death. The monster had gained by daring, that he
"might enjoy the hoard of rings at his own pleasure.
"Wælse's son loaded the sea-boat, bare bright ornaments
"into the ship's bosom. Heat melted the worm. He was
"far the greatest of wanderers, through the human race, the
"refuge of warriors. Therefore at first he throve by valiant
"deeds. After Heremod's war, labour and valour had
"ceased, he was forth betrayed, amongst the Eotens, into
"the power of his foes, quickly exiled The waves of sor-
"row afflicted him long; he became a life-long care to his
"people, to all his nobles. So oft in former times, many a
"prudent man,—who trusted to him for deliverance from
"evils, (trusted) that the chieftain's son should thrive, in-
"herit his father's honours, rule his people, his hoard, and
"refuge-city, the kingdom of heroes, the patrimony of the
"Scyldings,—bemourned the adventures of the bold-hearted
"one."[18]

Heremod may have been the immediate successor of Healfdene. Heorogar's succession only is mentioned; he must

---

[18] F. 149.

have reigned but a short time, and although he left a son Heoroweard, the kingdom came to his brother Hrothgar.

"Then was to Hrothgar given success in battle, the glory
"of war, so that his dear kinsmen gladly obeyed him, until
"that the youth waxed, a great kindred band."[19]

Another defect in the MS. deprives us of the means of knowing the fate of these princes, and the reason why Hrothgar was preferred to his nephew, for preferred he certainly was, and that by Heorogar. For Hrothgar, giving a sword and suit of armour to Beowulf:—

"Said that king Hiorogar, lord of the Scyldings, had it a
"long while. He would not give these breast-weeds in
"preference to his son, the bold Heoroweard, though he was
"dear to him."[20]

Twelve years before the date of the principal event in the poem, therefore about A.D. 495—

"It came into his mind that he would command men to
"construct a palace, a great mead-hall, which the sons of
"men should speak of for ever; and therein distribute to
"young and old, all such as God had given him, except the
"folk-share, and the lives of men. Then I have heard that
"the work was widely proclaimed to many a tribe through-
"out the earth, that a folk-stead was being adorned. In time
"it befel him, soon among men, that it was all ready, the
"greatest of palaces. He gave it the name Heort."[21]

This I have no doubt is Hart in Durham. Its situation, about two miles from the coast, agrees very well with the distance of Heort from the shore, indicated in the poem; and it is just the distance from the coast of Suffolk, Hygelac's territory, for Beowulf's voyage to have been accomplished in

---

[19] F. 130.   [20] F. 177.   [21] F. 130.

the time specified. Indeed the identity of Heort with Hart seems to be established beyond question, by a passage in Canto xx., taken in connection with these, and other circumstances, to be noticed in the sequel. A mere is mentioned—

"Where the *hill-stream* flows downward under the shades
"of the cliffs, the flood under the earth. It is not far hence,
"*a mile of distance*, that the mere stands, over which hang
"barky groves. *There lives not one so wise of the sons of*
"*men, who knows the bottom.*"[22]

At just this distance from Hart, there was, until lately, a large pool, called the *Bottomless Carr*, from which a stream, the "hill-stream" of the poem, still designated by the equivalent name *How-beck*, flowed through the parish of Hart into the Slake of Hartlepool, and still flows, though the pool has been drained, and converted into arable land. Thus the name of the pool and of the stream, and the distance from Hart, exactly correspond with the scene described in the poem; and if there be not a reference in the lines which follow :—

"although the heath-stepper, the hart mighty of horns,
"wearied by hounds, driven from afar, seek the holt-wood,
"sooner will he give up his soul, his life upon the brink, than
"he will (plunge) therein his head,"—

to the story, from which the name of Hartlepool, (Heruteu, "the water of the hart," Hiartapoll, Hert-in-pole) originated, and which is represented on the common seal of the borough, (a hart, standing in water, and attacked by a hound), it must be admitted that the coincidence is remarkable. The lines which follow these, again, relating the progress of Hrothgar and his thanes, as they tracked Grendel's mother along the

[22] F. 160.

coast, particularly those two which speak of "precipitous "cliffs, many nicor-houses," exactly describe the coast of Hartlepool, and its wave-worn caves.

At Hart there are traces of an ancient fort, including an area of about two acres, bounded by the Howbeck on the south; and, about a hundred yards to the south-west, there is an enclosure, called the Palace Garths. We have no intimation of the historic kings of Northumbria having ever resided at Hart; and as the proximity of the Palace Garths to the fort certainly indicates a royal residence, we have here an additional circumstance, in support of our conjecture, that Hart was the residence of Hrothgar.

Shortly, as it seems, after its construction, the fortress of Heort was attacked by the Beards, led by Withergyld, Frode, and Ingeld his son.

"The hall arose, high and horn-curved. It awaited the "war-tempest of hated fire. Nor was it long thenceforth, "ere the warrior commanded them to swear with oaths."[23]

"My friend thou mayest know the sword, the dear iron, "which thy father bare to the fight, under his closed helmet, "for the last time, when the Danes, the bold Scyldings, slew "him, gained the battle-field, after Withergyld fell, after "the overthrow of heroes."[24]

These however we could not have understood precisely, but for the clearer notice of the same affair in the Traveller's Tale.

"Hrothwulf and Hrothgar, paternal cousins, held longest "peace together, after they had repulsed the race of Wi- "cings, and defeated Ingeld's army, slaughtered at Heort "the host of the warlike Beards."[25]

---

[23] F. 130.   [24] F. 175.   [25] L. 91-100.

The neighbourhood of Hart actually presents the traces of a battle such as this. Near the north-western extremity of the Slake of Hartlepool, a number of holes have been found, about five feet below the surface, each filled with human bones, and about eight feet square;[26] and one grave, opened in 1851, contained the bodies of one hundred and fifty men of tall stature. The custom of most Teutonic tribes, in the days of Paganism, was undoubtedly to burn the bodies of the illustrious dead, but those of inferior rank, especially when slain in battle, would be buried; and the occurrence of so many graves, each containing several bodies, is most readily accounted for by the supposition of some battle, of which the tradition is lost, having been fought in the neighbourhood.

The first of the passages cited above, seems to imply that a peace was concluded between Hrothgar and Ingeld, as on a similar occasion between Fin and Hencgest.

Ingeld's principality appears to have been in the neighbouring county of York, where three Inglebys, Ingleton, and Ingleborough, bear his name, as Wycliffe, Barton, and Barforth on the Tees, do those of the Wycs (or Wycings) and Beards.

The hostility of a ferocious giant, named Grendel, is said to have been the occasion of terror of Hrothgar's people for the space of twelve years. Discarding of course, as exaggerations, all the marvellous circumstances of this part of the story, I still believe it had some foundation in fact. Grendel is certainly the name of a man; it occurs in the composition of the names of places, in such a way as to leave no doubt on this point. Not only do we find it in the names of Grendlesmere[27] in Wiltshire, and Grindelespytt[28] in Worcestershire, to which the

---

[26] Sir C. Sharp's History of Hartlepool.   [27] C. D. 353.
[28] C. D. 59.

late Mr. Kemble thought that some association with traditions, like the story in question, had given origin; but in that of Grindleton in Yorkshire, and Crindale dykes[29] on the Roman wall. Near to the latter there is Grindon lough and Grandy's knowe; and in the neighbourhood of Hart there is a parish named Grindon, and Grandy's close, all apparently bearing the name of the same person,—once no doubt a powerful chieftain settled in the county of Durham; and, singularly enough, in close proximity to Grandy's close, there is Thrum's law, *i. e.* the "giant's hill."

We are introduced to the court of Hrothgar, at the time of Beowulf's visit for the purpose of combating this giant. Hrothwulf, his cousin, is there; and the poet, confirming the statement in the Traveller's Tale, says, "as yet was their "peace together." Hrothgar's queen is Wealhtheow, of the family of the Helmings, the mother of two sons, Hrethric and Hrothmund, and of a daughter Freaware. Ingeld the son of Frode, prince of the Beards, is a visitor at his court, an accepted suitor for the hand of Freaware; and it was hoped that this alliance would be the means of effacing the memory of the old feud, and securing peace between the tribes:—

"Whiles Hrothgar's daughter, before the nobles, bare the
"ale-cup to the warriors in order, whom I heard those sitting
"in the hall, where she gave bright treasure to the heroes,
"name Freaware. Young, decked with gold, she was
"espoused to the glad son of Frode. Therefore hath he, the
"shepherd of his kingdom, become a friend of the Scyldings,
"and that rumour tells, that with the wife he has allayed a
"deal of death-feuds and conflicts."[30]

---

[29] Gryndeldikes in an old deed, quoted by Mr. Longstaffe.
[30] F. 174.

This, however, it was not, for the poet puts a prophetic speech, (his way of relating subsequent events), into the mouth of Beowulf, predicting that an old warrior would stir up in the breast of Ingeld the remembrance of his father's fall, by calling his attention to his sword, carried about the palace by Hrothgar's son; that Ingeld would murder the prince, make his escape, renounce his bride, and renew the war:—

" Yet seldom anywhere does the fatal spear rest, even for
" a little while, after a people's fall, although the bride be
" good. Therefore the prince of the warlike Beards, when
" he goeth about the palace, and every thane of their people,
" may think of that; when the royal child of the Danes,
" served by nobles, rejoices to gird on himself the hard and
" ringed sword, the legacy of the ancients, the treasure of the
" warlike Beards, whilst they might wield their weapons,
" until they misled their dear comrades, and their own lives,
" to the linden-play. Then an old spear-warrior, who beholds
" the ring, who remembers all the war-slaughter of men, will
" say at the beer; fierce will be his spirit, sad of mood will he
" begin, through his bosom's thought, to try the mind of
" the young warrior, to wake the plague of war and
" will say that word; ' My friend, thou mayest know the
" ' sword,' &c.

" So will he excite and remind him, every time, with
" mournful words, until the occasion come, that the fated
" thane, after the bite of the bill, shall sleep blood-stained,
" deprived of life, for his father's deeds. Thence the other
" warrior will escape, he knows the land well. Then the
" sworn oaths of warriors will be broken on both sides.
" Deadly hatred will afterwards boil in Ingeld, and the love

"of his wife will become cooler, after the waves of care.
"Therefore I do not consider the alliance of the warlike
"Beards, their part of lordly kinship with the Danes reliable,
"(nor) their friendship fast."[31]

The victim of Ingeld's revenge seems to have been Hrothmund; for, in another prospective speech, Beowulf speaks of Hrethric, as coming to the Geats to seek aid, and of himself as being allowed by Hygelac to conduct an army of auxiliaries:—

"If that I hear, over the course of the floods, that they
"who dwell around thee urge thee with terror, as, hating
"thee, they whiles have done, I shall soon be ready. I will
"bring to thee thousands of thanes, of heroes to help. I
"know of Hygelac, the lord of the Geats, though he be
"young, the shepherd of his people, that he will, by words
"and works, enable me, that I may defend thee well, and bear
"to thine aid the spear-forest, the support of thy power, if
"thou have need of men. If then Hrethric, the king's son,
"shall repair to the courts of the Geats, he may find many
"friends there."[32]

Another of these speeches, assigned to Wealhtheow, intimates that, when Hrothgar died, his cousin Hrothwulf, who was much younger than he, succeeded him, and repaid the kindness he had received from them in his youth, by protecting their son Hrethric:—

"When thou shalt go forth to see the Godhead, I know
"my glad Hrothwulf, that he will maintain the youth with
"honour, if thou, friend of the Scyldings, leavest the world
"before him. I ween that he will repay our son with good,
"if he remembereth well what benefits we two performed

---

[31] F. 174, 175.   [32] F. 170.

"for his pleasure and dignity, formerly when he was a "child."[33]

Allusion is afterwards made to the extinction of Hrothgar's race in war, and to Beowulf's being called to reign over the Scyldings.

Such is the history of a family who appear to have originally settled in the districts north of the wall, afterwards borne part in the enterprise of Horsa and Hencgest, and eventually moved southward, and occupied the southern division of what is now the county of Durham. In this district we have several traces of the persons who are mentioned in connection with them. The Helmings, the family of Wealhtheow, have given their name to Helmington; and the Secgas, subjects of Healfdene, to Sedgefield, about six miles from Hart. Naisbury about a mile south of Hart, and Neasham on the Tees, may have derived their names from Hnæf, Healfdene's vassal, who fell at Finnesham; and Elwick, Elstol, Elton, and Eldon, all in South Durham, and the first and last near Hart, theirs from the Scylfing Ela, who is mentioned at the commencement of the poem, after the notice of Hrothgar's sons.

Beowulf the Scylding is said to have reigned in the Scedelands, and Scedenig, (probably the island near the coast, the destruction of which is alluded to in the days of Beowulf the Geat), is named as a residence of Hrothgar. Doubtless these two names have a common derivation, and Mr. Kemble has rightly translated *scedelandum in* "in the divided lands." *Sceadan* and *sundrian* have the same signification, "to divide" or "separate;" and these Scedelands appear to be represented

---

[33] F. 156.

by the modern Sunderlands, of which one is on the coast of Northumberland, north of Shilbottle, two in Durham, one in Cumberland, and one in Yorkshire. As used in this poem, the word perhaps means the lands which were apportioned to this race at their first coming; and, (like other words now applied to parishes), once designated districts of considerable extent.

It is observed that Ingeld's knowledge of the country is said to have favoured his escape, a circumstance confirmatory of the supposition that his home was in Yorkshire, his territory bordering on Hrothgar's.

All these circumstances considered, we can have no doubt of the correctness of our theory, which assigns to these princes of the Scyldings a kingdom on the coast of Northumbria, and identifies Heort with Hart. Our Healfdene, Hrothgar, and Halga, are not to be confounded with Halfdan, Hroar, and Helgi, of the Norse genealogy, whom a collation of the genealogies proves to have lived several generations later, and whose pedigree differs from theirs in every other respect. Beowulf the grandfather, and Heorogar the elder brother, of Hrothgar are equally unknown to Danish tradition; in the genealogy, Hrolf is the son of Helgi and nephew of Hroar; in the poem, Hrothwulf is the cousin of Hrothgar by the father's side. Saxo perhaps was acquainted with the story of our Hrothgar, and so incorporated with his history the building of Roskeldia, in "his laudable anxiety to connect in one work, for the "honour of his fatherland, all the legends which he found "here and there current, respecting any princes of the "Teutonic stock."[34]

---

[34] Kemble, Preface to Beowulf, II. p. xxxi.

CHAPTER III.

The Fight at Finnesham.

IT is in this poem we find the earliest notice of the second Hencgest, who appears for the first time in our history in A.D. 444.

If we take strictly the chronological indications it supplies, of the length of Hrothgar's reign, it would appear that he succeeded to the throne about A.D. 445, and had reigned sixty-two years[1] at the time of Beowulf's visit to his court. We may therefore presume that the interval, between his accession and the death of Healfdene, which was occupied by the reigns of Heremod and Heorogar, was not long. This, however, is not of much

---

[1] As Healfdene's war-chiefs, however, were living at the time of Beowulf's visit, there seems to be a sort of necessity to suppose a shorter duration for Hrothgar's reign. *Hund* may have originally signified the number to which it is first attached in the Anglo-Saxon system of numeration, *i.e.* "seventy;" or it may have been "sixty-four," eight times eight, as eight was the sacred number. If so, the *hund missera*, of which Hrothgar speaks, would be thirty-five or thirty-two years, previous to the twelve years' persecution of Grendel. This would place his accession in A.D. 460 or 463, forty-seven or forty-four years before Beowulf's visit, which is far more probable.

consequence, since the title, " Healfdene's hero," given to Hnæf in one of the following passages, does not necessarily imply that the events, in which he took part, occurred in Healfdene's lifetime; for the song is said to have been sung " before Healfdene's war-chiefs," and that was at the time of Beowulf's visit. It is probable, however, that they did occur during his reign, or at any rate before Hrothgar's accession.

It seems to me almost certain, that the hero of the story is not the first Hencgest, who led the Angles to Britain. He is called the " prince's thane," and so might our Hencgest be called until A.D. 434, when he succeeded his brother as king of Kent, but of course not afterwards; and if Fin, as we have supposed, accompanied our Hencgest to Britain, this feud, in which he perished, could not have occurred before A.D. 428. Nor could it have occurred between that date and A.D. 434; for, besides that policy would dictate the necessity of preserving peace with his allies, whilst he was engaged in securing a firm footing in Britain, Hencgest's time, during these first six years of his residence in this country, appears to have been too actively occupied, to have left him leisure for a feud such as this, in which part of two years were spent. The first Hencgest, therefore, had nothing to do with it. After his expulsion and return to Britain, we have an interval of six years, from A.D. 437 to 443, when the Teutonic tribes, relieved from all fear of molestation on the part of the Britons, were at liberty to quarrel amongst themselves. To this interval the feud may with great probability be referred; and, as the hero cannot have been the first Hencgest, who was then a powerful king, we can have little hesitation in accepting the alternative, that he was the second Hencgest, of whom the Frisian traditions speak, the nephew of the first.

Hencgest I. had established his son Octa in Northumbria, and from Northumbria this Hencgest appears to have come, for he was associated in his enterprise with Hnæf of the Scyldings, whilst he was himself a chieftain of Eotens or Jutes. He was therefore a neighbour of the family who, as we have seen, reigned on the coast of Durham.

The Finnesham of the poem appears to be the place which still bears the name, in Norfolk; in the neighbourhood of which, (about nine miles distant), the name of Fin's queen, Hildeburh, occurs at Hillborough;[2] that of her father, Hoce, at Hockwold, (twelve miles from Finsham and nine from Hillborough), and at Hockham, (twenty miles farther to the south-west); and that of Guthhere, one of the heroes of this expedition, at Gooderstone.

It is not a little remarkable, that of the very few fragments which remain of the heroic poems of our forefathers, one, (which survived the almost universal destruction of these monuments of antiquity, until it could be transcribed by a scholar who appreciated its value, and since his time has disappeared), relates to the same event, and supplies in part what is wanting in this episode. The narrative it contains is here placed after the introductory lines to the passage in Beowulf, which presents to us a picture of the mode in which the memory of the exploits of their heroes was preserved amongst our forefathers, and the recital thereof entertained them at their feasts.

" There was song and sound all together, the joy-wood

---

[2] " Hildeburh wella," Domesday.

" touched, the lay oft sung, before Healfdene's war-chiefs;
" when Hrothgar's minstrel, the joy of the hall, should tell
" about Fin's sons, when the invasion came upon them,
" (when) Healfdene's hero, Hnæf of the Scyldings, should
" fall in Frisian slaughter."[3]

The fragment introduces the Frisian king arousing his followers, on seeing the light of the fire, which his enemies had kindled for the destruction of his castle.

" Then the warlike young king cried aloud, 'This dawns
" ' not from the east, nor does a dragon fly here, nor are the
" ' horns of this hall burning; but here it blazes forth, the
" ' fowls sing, the cricket chirps, the war-wood resounds,
" ' shield answers to shaft. Now shines the moon, wander-
" ' ing under the welkin. Now deeds of woe arise, that this
" ' people's enmity will do. But wake up now, my warriors,
" ' hold your land, think of valour, march in array, be una-
" ' nimous.' Then many a gold-decked thane arose, girded
" on his sword. Then noble champions went to the door,
" Sigeferth and Eaha drew their swords, and at the other
" doors Ordlaf and Guthlaf and Hengest himself turned on
" their track. Then yet Guthhere upbraided Garulf, that he,
" so noble a soul, bare not arms to the hall-doors the first
" time, now a fierce enemy would take it. But he, the
" fierce-minded warrior, inquired above all publicly, who
" held the door? 'Sigeferth is my name,' quoth he, 'I am
" ' prince of the Secgas, a leader widely known. I have en-
" ' dured many woes, hard battles; for thee is yet here
" ' decreed, whatever thou thyself wilt seek from me.' Then
" was the din of slaughter in the hall. The keeled-board
" should —— (the sword) they took in hand to break the

[3] F. 153.

"bone-helm.[4] The castle-floor resounded, until in the fight, Garulf, Guthhere's son, fell first of all earthdwellers. The corpses of many good foes surrounded him. The raven wandered, swarthy and sallow-brown. Never did I hear of sixty victorious heroes more worthily, better bear them at a conflict of men, nor ever so[5] —— nor better repay for white mead, than his bachelors requited Hnæf. They fought five days, so that none of them, of the noble companions, fell, but they held the door. Then the wounded hero (Hnæf) betook him to go away, said that his byrnie was broken, his wardress weak, and also that his helm was pierced. Then the shepherd of his people soon inquired of him, how the warriors recovered of their wounds."

The sequel is in Beowulf.

"Hildeburh at least had no cause to praise the Eotens' compact. She was bereaved of the guiltless ones, her beloved children and brothers, at the war-play; they fell in succession, wounded by the spear. That was an afflicted

---

[4]   "Sceolde celod bord
        "genumon handa
        "bán-helm berstan."

Mr. Kemble suggests the possibility that some lines are lost, as the metre is defective; and this I believe is the case. As an alternative, he ventures a correction, "sceolde næglod bord genumen handa." Mr. Thorpe proposes "sceolde nalæs bord genumen handa," and his translation of the following line, "they lacked the bone-helm," would require another word to be altered, "berstan" into "burston." Where an error is evident, and the substitution of a word restores sense to an unintelligible passage, we may generally accept the emendation; but not when the alteration of a word requires other alterations, as in this case.

[5]   "Ne nefre swâ
        "noc hwítne medo
        "sél forgyldan."

Here again I suspect that something is wanting. Mr. Thorpe proposes "ne næfre sang ne hwítne medo."

"lady. Not in vain did Hoce's daughter mourn their death, after morning came, when she might see under heaven the slaughter of her kinsmen, where she held before most of the world's joy. War took away all Fin's thanes, save a few only, so that he might not in any wise contend with Hencgest at the meeting-place, nor defend by war the sad remnant from the prince's thane. But they offered him conditions, that they should yield to him wholly another palace, a hall and throne; that they should have half power with the sons of the Eotens, and that Folcwalda's son, every day, at the gifts of money, should honour the Danes, Hencgest's band, should grace them with rings, with hoard-treasures of solid gold, even as much as he would supply to the race of Frisians in the beer-hall. Then they pledged a fast covenant of peace on both sides. Fin, boldly, peaceably, undertook with oaths to Hencgest, that he would honourably maintain the sad remnant[6] by the doom of his witan; so that no man, by words or deeds, should break the treaty, nor ever remind (them) through wicked device, though princeless they must follow the slayer of their ring-giver, since so they were obliged. If then any one of the Frisians should make mention of that murder-feud with insolent speech, then the edge of the sword should punish it afterwards. The oath was taken on both sides, and much gold raised from the hoard.

"The best of warriors, of the warlike Scyldings, was ready on the pile. The gore-stained sark, the swine all-golden, the boar iron-hard, were easily seen at the pile; many a noble crippled with wounds; some had fallen in the battle.

---

[6] Hnæf's band.

"Hildeburh then commanded her own son to be involved in flame, to burn his body at Hnæf's pile, and to place the wretched one on his shoulder on the pile. The lady mourned, lamented in songs. The warrior ascended, whirled to the clouds; the greatest of death-fires roared before the mound. The mail-hoods melted, the wound-gates burst; then the blood sprang forth, the loathly bite of the corpse. Flame, greediest of spirits, devoured all those whom there war took away. The glory of both nations was departed.

"The warriors then, deprived of friends, betook them to visit the dwellings, to see Frysland, the homes and lofty city. Hencgest there yet abode with Fin, through the death-hued winter. He tilled the land peaceably, though he might drive the ringed prow on the sea. The sea boiled with storms, wan against the wind; winter locked the wave with icy bond, until that another year came to the dwellings. So now doth yet that which constantly happily provideth glory-bright weather. Then was winter departed, the bosom of the earth fair. The exile departed, the guest from the dwellings. He thought more of vengeance than of a sea-voyage, if he might contrive a hostile meeting, since he inly remembered the sons of the Eotens. So he did not shun worldly counsel, when he placed on his bosom Hunlafing, the flame of war, the best of swords. For there were among the Eotens men known for the sword, and bold of spirit. Savage sword-slaughter afterwards overwhelmed Fin at his own home; when Guthlaf and Oslaf, after the sea-voyage, sadly remembered the grim onset, considered their portion of sorrows. He might not restrain in his breast his wavering mood. Then was the

"hall surrounded by the hosts of his foes, Fin also slain, the
"king amongst his troop, and the queen taken. The shooters
"of the Scyldings bare to the ships all the household wealth,
"of jewels and mounted gems, of the earth-king, such as
"they might find at Finnesham. They bare the noble lady
"on the sea-way to the Danes, led her to their people."[7]

---

[7] F. 153-155.

CHAPTER IV.

Hygelac and his Family.

YGELAC was the son of Hrethel, and nephew of Swerting. Hrethel, whose name occurs in this poem alone, was probably one of the associates of Hencgest; and, from the traces that remain of his name, we may infer that he resided for a time in Yorkshire, (where Seomel, his father or father-in-law, reigned), and afterwards removed to Suffolk.

For we have several places which bear the name of his subjects, the Weders; in Suffolk itself, two Wetherdens, Weatherheath, Wetherup, and Wetheringsett; and in the adjoining county of Cambridge Wetherley hundred; and one which bears the name of his family, Redlingfield, in Suffolk. His own name appears at Rattlesden and Rattlerow hill, in the same county; the etymology of the latter, *Hrædlan hræw*, suggesting the idea that it was his place of sepulture.

About a mile distant from one of the Wetherdens, there is an ancient fortress, of the usual plan of Anglo-Saxon strongholds, called Haughley, which may have been the residence of this family. In its name, (when we consider its variations[1]), we may even trace that of Hygelac himself. This is a name which we cannot expect to meet with, otherwise than in a corrupted or abbreviated form; and it is therefore by no means surprising, that we can find no name on the map of Suffolk which can be positively said to contain it. There is one, however, respecting which I think there can be little doubt, Hoxne. In Brompton's time it was Hoxton, but he says that its ancient name was Eglesdon or Halesdon. Wendover calls it Haeilesdune, and Leland, quoting from a Life of S. Eadmund, Hegilesdune. If we suppose it Hygelácesdún, the transition to its present name is easy; but it is impossible to conceive the process by which Halesdun could become Hoxton. It is about four miles to the north of Redlingfield. Uggeshall, farther to the east, may be a corruption of Hygdesheál, Hygd having been, as it appears, another name of Hygelac.[2]

---

[1] Huiglauc, Hugleikr, Chocilaic.

[2] Prof. Leo, and Messrs. Ettmüller and Thorpe, have taken Hygd to be the name of Hæreth's daughter, Hygelac's queen; Mr. Kemble, on the contrary, regarded it as another name of Hygelac. I follow Mr. Kemble for these reasons:—

1. To take the passage, which speaks of Hæreth's daughter, (f. 172), in continuation of what is said of Hygd, seems, (as Mr. K. has remarked), to make nonsense of the whole; to take it separately, and suppose that the lines, which connected it with what precedes it, are lost, renders it perfectly intelligible in itself. No more than one or two couplets are necessary, to connect this notice of the queen with that of her husband.

2. The parallel is exact between,—

"The building was excellent, the king a famous prince,"
and
"the hall high, Hygd very young, wise, well-established,"—
and the king must be Hygd.

3. The meaning of Hygd is the same as that of the first part of Hygelac's name, and it would be appropriate as a second name for him. We have several instances of simple and compound names being borne by the same person.

Hrethel's family consisted of three sons, Herebeald, Hæthcyn, and Hygelac, and a daughter, not named, who was given in marriage to Ecgtheow. He died of grief for the loss of his eldest son, as related in the following passage:—

"The deathbed was strewed for the eldest unfitly, by the
"act of his kinsman, when Hæthcyn, his lord-friend, slew him
"with an arrow from his horn-bow; he missed his mark and
"shot his kinsman, one brother another, with a bloody shaft.
"That was a priceless slaughter, horribly done. Hrethel
"was weary of heart. Nevertheless the ætheling must part
"from life unavenged. It would be so sad for the old man
"to endure, that his young son should ride upon the gallows.
"So the helm of the Weders bore boiling heart-sorrow for
"Herebeald. He might in no wise avenge the feud on the
"slayer, nor on account of it hate the warrior with hostile
"deeds, though it was not pleasing to him. He then for
"sorrow, since this woe befel him, gave up the joy of men,
"chose God's light; left to his sons, (as a happy man doth),
"his land and royal city, when he departed from life."[3]

Here it seems to be clearly expressed, that the old man's affection for his surviving son withheld him from avenging the feud; and that it was priceless, because the weregild was not demanded, rather than because the laws of the Geats exacted none under such circumstances.[4]

Hæthcyn, (whose name may possibly be traced in that of Akenham about twelve miles from Rattlesden), and Hygelac

---

4. Beowulf received a beautiful collar, at Hrothgar's court, from Wealhtheow, and gave it to Hygd on his return home; Hygelac wore it in his last conflict with the Franks; it seems therefore that Hygd and Hygelac are one.

[3] F. 184.   [4] As Mr. Thorpe has understood it.

appear to have reigned conjointly on the death of their father. Immediately, as it seems, after their accession, they undertook an expedition against the Sweos, which is thus related in two passages of the poem. The first immediately follows that just quoted:—

" There was quarrel and strife, mutual dissension, fierce
" hatred of warriors, of the Sweos and Geats, over the wide
" water, after Hrethel died; until to him Ongentheow's sons
" were——"

Here there is a hiatus in the MS.; what followed perhaps related to the war which Beowulf waged with the Scylfings, at a later time.

" Brave, fierce in war, they would not hold peace over the
" deep, but oft they completed the terrible ambush around
" Hreosnabeorh. (That feud and offence my friend may re-
" late, as it was known). War was busy for Hæthcyn, the
" lord of the Geats, although the other bought with his life a
" hard bargain. Then, on the morrow, I have heard, the
" other kinsman stole on the slayer, with edges of the sword.
" There Ongentheow attacks Eofer.[5] His war-helm glided
" off, the old Scylfing fell pale. He remembered his hand
" and the feud full well, he withheld not the fatal blow."[6]

The foregoing passage is necessary to the complete understanding of some parts of the following, in which we have fuller and clearer details of this campaign. The poet makes

---

[5] " Thær Ongentheów There Ongentheow
" Eofores niosath." visits Eofer.
Mr. Thorpe suggests the following alteration of these lines,—
" Thær wæs Ongentheów There was Ongentheow
" Eofores nithes sæd." sated with Eofer's enmity.
[6] F. 185.

Beowulf, who is the speaker in the foregoing, refer to his friend's knowledge of the circumstances of the history, (" my " friend may relate "); and accordingly he represents one of Beowulf's warriors, after his death, as saying, *inter alia*:—

" Nor do I in any wise expect peace or fidelity from the
" Sweofolk. For it was widely known, that Ongentheow
" deprived Hæthcyn, the Hrethling, of life, beside Raven-
" wood; when, for pride, the Geats' people first sought the
" warlike Scylfings. Soon to him the prudent, old, and
" terrible father of Ohthere dealt a hand-blow. The sea-
" leader, the old man, long before, had borne away, from the
" bridal-hearth, the maid decked with gold, the mother of
" Onela and Ohthere; and then he followed his deadly foes,
" until they escaped with difficulty into Ravensholt, deprived
" of their lord. Then he beset the escaped of the swords,
" weary with wounds, with a mighty force. Oft he threatened
" woe, all night long, to the wretched race; said that he
" would take them in the morning with edges of the sword;
" hang some on gallows-tree for sport. Much comfort came,
" together with the dawn of day, to the sad of mood, after
" they heard Hygelac's horns and trumpets sound; when the
" good king came faring after them, with the force of his
" people. The bloody trace of the Sweos and Geats, the
" deadly rush of men, how the people excited feud with them,
" was widely seen. The good (king) then betook him with
" his comrades, prudent and very sorrowful, to seek (his)
" fortress; the warrior Ongentheow went higher; he had
" heard of Hygelac's warfare, the proud chief's battle-craft;
" he trusted not that he could repel his foe's seamen, the war-
" like voyagers, defend his treasure, his children, and his
" bride. Thence again the old man withdrew under the

"earth-wall. Then was treasure offered by the Sweos'
"people, an ensign to Hygelac.'[7] Then they passed forth
"over the peaceful plain. The Hrethlings afterwards
"thronged to the rampart. Then was hope destroyed for
"Ongentheow, the grey-haired, with edges of the sword; so
"that the king of the people should yield to Eofer's doom
"alone. Wulf Wonreding angrily reached him with his
"weapon, so that, for the blow, blood sprang forth from the
"veins, under his hair. Yet the old Scylfing was not dis-
"mayed, but quickly repaid that deadly attack with a worse
"exchange. The swift son of Wonred could not give a
"hand-blow to the old man, after the king of the people
"turned towards him, for he beforehand cut through the
"helmet on his head, so that he must bow, blood-stained; he
"fell on the earth. Yet he was not doomed, although the
"wound disabled him, but he recovered himself. Then the
"fierce thane of Hygelac let his broad falchion, his old
"Eotenish sword, break the giant helmet over the shield-
"wall, where his brother lay. Then sank the king, the
"shepherd of his people, his life was stricken. There were
"many who rescued his kinsman, they raised him up quickly,
"when room was made for them, that they might command
"the battle-field, when one warrior stripped another. They
"took from Ongentheow his iron-byrnie, his hard-hilted
"sword, and his helmet together; they bare to Hygelac the
"armour of the hoary warrior. He received the war-gear,
"and fairly promised them rewards among the people, and
"so he performed. The lord of the Geats, the son of

---

[7] The "ensign to Hygelac" corresponds to the modern flag of truce; and the "peaceful plain" was the space left unoccupied by the opposed forces, while proposals for peace were under consideration.

"Hrethel, when he came home, paid Eofer and Wulf for the battle-onslaught. Besides treasures, he gave to either of them a hundred thousand of land, and locked rings; nor needed any man on earth upbraid them for the gift, since they won glory in battle. And then he gave to Eofer his only daughter, a dignity to his home, a pledge of affection."[8]

From these two passages we learn, that Ongentheow long before had carried off Hæthcyn's bride, who became his queen, and the mother of his sons Onela and Ohthere; and that, immediately after the death of their father, Hæthcyn and Hygelac led an armament over sea, to avenge the feud.[9] They appear to have divided their forces; Hæthcyn's division was attacked by Ongentheow, suffered defeat with the loss of their leader, and fled into Ravenwood, where Ongentheow beset them all night, threatening to exterminate them on the morrow. At daybreak, however, Hygelac's division arrived to their rescue. A second battle ensued, resulting in the discomfiture of Ongentheow, who withdrew up the country to his fortress, Hreosnabeorh, pursued by the Hrethlings. The Sweos offered their treasures as the price of peace, but in vain. In the assault upon the fortress, Ongentheow, attacked and wounded by Wulf, dealt him in return a severe though not mortal wound, and then fell by the hand of Eofer.

---

[8] F. 193, 194.

[9] The whole context shows that this was an aggression on the part of the Geats, their first; for the origin of the feud, a previous expedition of Ongentheow and the Scylfings, is spoken of. So the reading, "when the Scylfings first sought the Geats," (which is, besides, inconsistent with the statements relative to Ongentheow's withdrawing to a fortress after his defeat, the Geats following him, the Sweos offering their treasures, and Hygelac's return home), is out of the question.

Hygelac, on his return home, rewarded the valour of the two brothers, by giving to each a large grant of land, and to Eofer the hand of his daughter in marriage.

Whether this battle was fought on the continent or in England, does not of course affect the question of the home of Hrethel and Hygelac; but I think it very probable that it was in this country. Norse traditions, indeed, mention an Angantyr, king of Sweden, but his story differs altogether from that of our Ongentheow; and the mention of Sweoríce is not decisive, because wherever the Sweos established a kingdom, it would of course be Sweoríce. Now this was undoubtedly one of the races which settled in Britain; the Scylfings have left their name to Shilvington in Northumberland; and the mention of this race, in the midst of details relative to Hrothgar's family, renders it probable that they were his neighbours. Accordingly, it is in the district which borders on his territories, that I find the scenes of this campaign. The first battle was fought in the neighbourhood of a wood, which is called Hrefnes-holt and Hrefna-wudu; the former designation being derived from the name of Hræfn, the latter indicating that of his family, the Hræfnas or Hræfningas, of whom we have several traces in this country, and one of them at Ravenhill, on the coast of Yorkshire, near Whitby. The position of this Ravenhill suggests the probability that the adjacent Robin Hood's bay may really be a corruption of Ravenwood bay.[10] In this neighbourhood the first battle may have been fought; and War dyke to the south, and the Green dyke to the east, of Ravenhill, may be

---

[10] The similarity of names having occasioned the memory of this popular hero to be connected, not only with the bay, but with the ancient tumuli near Ravenhill, Robin Hood's butts.

the remains of entrenchments, which the fugitives constructed to defend their position from the threatened attack of Ongentheow. Six miles to the north-west is a village, Ugglebarnby, which seems to bear the name of Hygelac, and may mark the scene of the second battle; close to it appears to have been a place called Brecca,[11] the name of a neighbour of Hygelac; and about twenty miles farther to the west is Roseberry Topping,[12] a lofty precipitous hill, around the conical summit of which a complete circle of large pits is supposed to mark the dwellings of a primitive race. This, I believe, is Hreosnabeorh, the fortress to which Ongentheow retired after the battle with Hygelac, in the defence of which he lost his life. The close of the fifth century, or beginning of the sixth, may be assigned as the date of this feud.

As this was certainly the period of Hygelac's reign, it is exceedingly probable that he would be confederate with Garmund in the war against the Britons, and so may have given his name to Hygeláces git[13] near Clifton in Somersetshire, Hucklecote near Gloucester, and Hugglescote near Charley in Leicestershire, both of which neighbourhoods were scenes of this war.

Three passages in the poem allude to Hygelac's death:—

"That ring Hygelac of the Geats, Swerting's nephew, had
" for the last time, when he defended the treasure under his
" banner, guarded the spoil of the slain. Fate took him
" away, when he for pride sought woe, feud with the Fri-
" sians. He, the powerful prince, carried the ornament, the
" precious stones, over the cup of waves. He fell beneath

---

[11] Domesday.

[12] Rosedale, a valley to the south-east of this hill, bears the name of the same race.   [13] Cod. Diplom. 566.

"his shield. Then the king's life, his breast-weeds, and the
"ring together, departed into the grasp of the Franks.
"Worse warriors plundered the fallen, after the lot of war.
"The people of the Geats held the home of the dead."[14]

"That was not the least of contests, when they slew Hy-
"gelac; when the king of the Geats, the lordly friend of
"the people, the son of Hrethel, perished in war-onsets,
"sword drunken, beaten down by a bill, in the Frislands."[15]

"Now there is expectation to the people of a time of war,
"when the fall of the king becomes known among the Franks
"and Frisians. The feud was formed, fierce with the Hugas,
"when Hygelac came faring with a fleet to Frisland; there
"the Hetwaras overcame him in war. Boldly they came
"with over-might, so that the mailed warrior must bow, he
"fell in battle, the chieftain gave no treasure to his no-
"bles."[16]

This unfortunate expedition of Hygelac[17] is recorded by Gregory of Tours, and in the "Gesta Regum Francorum." The former[18] tells us, that in the beginning of the reign of

---

[14] F. 156   [15] F. 182.   [16] F. 193.

[17] This Hygelac is not to be confounded with his namesake, Hugleikr, king of Sweden, who fell in battle on Fyrisvellir, near Upsal. The latter, according to the Ynglinga Saga, was the son of Alf, an unwarlike character; his opponent was Hake, a viking who invaded his territory; and his two sons fell with him. He has therefore nothing in common with our Hygelac, but the name, and the circumstance that he also fell on the battle-field.

[18] "Dani cum rege suo, nomine Chocilaico, evectu navali per mare
"Gallias appetunt. Egressi ad terras, pagum unum de regno Theuderici
"devastant atque captivant; oneratisque navibus, tam de captivis quam
"de reliquis spoliis, reverti ad patriam cupiunt. Sed rex eorum in littus
"residebat, donec naves altum mare comprehenderent, ipse deinceps
"secuturus. Quod cum Theuderico nunciatum fuisset, quod scilicet

Theuderic, A.D. 511, the Danes with their king, Chocilaic, disembarked on the coast of Gaul; plundered and devastated a district belonging to Theuderic, filled their ships with the spoils, and with captives, and were preparing to return home, their king waiting on the shore, until the vessels could be got into deep water; that Theuderic, as soon as the intelligence reached him, sent his son Theudibert with a large force to attack him; and that he slew the king, defeated the Danes at sea, and recovered all the spoils. The narrative in the latter[19] is couched in nearly the same terms, but supplies one particular in addition; the name of the tribe who occupied the plundered district,—the Attoarii or Hetwaras. In the days of Tacitus, this tribe, whom he calls Chatuarii, occupied an island at the mouth of the Rhine; and on an island so situated, and perhaps the same, a writer of the tenth century[20] testifies, that the bones of Hygelac were preserved to his time, and shown to strangers on account of their gi-

---

" regio ejus fuerit ab extraneis devastata, Theudebertum, filium suum, in
" illas partes, cum magno exercitu ac magno armorum apparatu, direxit.
" Qui, interfecto rege, hostes navali prælio superatos opprimit, omnemque
" rapinam terræ restituit." H. F. III. 3.

[19] " In illo tempore, Dani cum rege suo, nomine Chochilago, cum
" navali hoste per altum mare Gallias appetunt, Theuderici pagum At-
" toarios, et alios devastantes, atque captivantes, plenas naves de captivis
" habentes, alto mare intrantes, rex eorum ad littus maris resedit. Quod
" cum Theuderico nunciatum fuisset, Theudebertum, filium suum, cum
" magno exercitu in illis partibus dirigens; qui, consequens eos, pug-
" navit cum eis cæde maximâ, atque ipsis prostratis regem eorum inter-
" fecit, prædam tulit, et in terram suam restituit." C. XIX.

[20] " De Huiglauco Getarum rege, miræ magnitudinis. Et sunt miræ
" magnitudinis, ut rex Huiglaucus, qui imperavit Getis, et a Francis
" occisus est; quem equus a duodecimo anno portare non potuit, cuius
" ossa in Rheni fluminis insulâ, ubi in oceanum prorumpit, asservata
" sunt, et de longinquo venientibus pro miraculo ostenduntur." MS.
Sæc. X. quoted by Moritz, Alt-Haupt-Deutsche Blätter.

gantic size. He also says, that he was king of the Getæ, and was slain by the Franks. The Chronicon Quedlinburgense supplies a further illustration of the passage, which speaks of the Hugas as Hygelac's adversaries, in designating the king of the Franks *Hugo* Theodoricus. These notices are very important, not only because they serve to fix the date of Hygelac's reign,—ending about the time of Theuderic's accession,—but also because their exact agreement with the passages in the poem which relate to the same event, warrants us in regarding the poem as in the main historical; since in the single instance, in which the light of authentic history is brought to bear upon it, it is found to be exactly accordant therewith.

Heardred, Hygelac's son, is called Hereric's nephew. Hereric was therefore probably the brother of Hygelac's queen. If we identify him with the Frank king, Chararic, we shall probably discover the occasion of the feud. Chararic, as well as other princes of the Frank blood royal, had been treacherously slain by Chlodovech; Garmund and Isembard, to revenge these murders, conducted an expedition to Gaul, and were defeated by Chlodovech, in the territory over which Chararic had reigned; and, about the same time, Hygelac, (whose probable connection with Garmund has been already noticed), landed in Theuderic's territory, immediately north of Chararic's, and after a successful foray, was slain by Theudebert. It is by no means improbable that these two expeditions were made each in conjunction with the other; that vengeance, for the murders of which Chlodovech had been guilty, was the motive of Hygelac, Chararic's brother-in-law, as it was of Isembard.

The probability that Hrethel, the brother or brother-in-law of Swerting,—whose father, Seomel, was the first of the ancestors of Ælle to establish himself in Northumbria,—was associated with them in their enterprise, and afterwards settled in Suffolk, where so many traces of his name, and of those of his family and people remain, (a probability which circumstances to be noticed in the next Chapter will be found to confirm), justifies us in claiming a place in our history for Hygelac; whose name is found, if not distinctly within the limits of his own principality, at any rate in other districts in which, from the circumstances of the times in which he lived, we might expect to find it. According to the genealogies he would be the cotemporary of Wilgils, between whom and Ælle there are two generations. He fell about A.D. 511, and Ælle became king of Deira in A.D. 558.

CHAPTER V.

The Story of Offa.

HE story of Offa, as preserved to us in this poem, in the Traveller's Tale, the Chronicle of John Rosse, and Matthew Paris' Life of him, now claims our attention. The two last are drawn from one source, the records of the monastery of S. Albans. Matthew Paris was a member of the community there; and John Rosse says, that he read the story there in a book "De Gestis Abbatum," and had seen it worked in tapestry on the walls of the abbot's hall. We might therefore expect to find these writers perfectly accordant, but it is not so; there are differences between them as to certain details, which, however, do not materially affect the story. It is to this effect.

When the Saxons had established themselves in Britain, (probably at the time of Hencgest's conquest, A. D. 441), they divided the land amongst themselves, appointing kings in different districts; and Wærmund received for his principality what is now called Warwickshire, repaired the town of Warwick, and gave his name to it. He had but one son, born to him when he was far advanced in years, of vigorous form, but blind until his seventh year, and deaf and dumb until his thirtieth. This defect was a source of great grief to the king and his nobles, for it was impossible to name the prince heir to the throne, and the age and infirmities of the king made it necessary to settle the succession. One of his nobles, who is called Rigan and Aliel, coveted it for his family, and was abetted by another, named Mitun. He petitioned the king to adopt him for his heir, and took care to intimate to him, through his partizans, that what he sought as a grace, would be extorted by force of arms, if refused. The old king was to be moved neither by entreaties nor by threats; he summoned his Witan, and their decision was adverse to the pretensions of Aliel, who consequently left the council in anger, and prepared for war. In a few days he had collected an army, and challenged Wærmund to battle. A second council was held to arrange matters, and Offa, who was present at their deliberations, suddenly acquired the faculty of hearing, so as to become cognizant of what was going on, and then that of speech. Aliel's friends, who were present, were confounded and retired; the rest besought Wærmund to confer on his son the insignia of knighthood; and Offa accordingly received them, along with several companions.

Both parties were now determined on war; the time and place for the encounter were fixed; and the forces of Offa and Aliel met on the opposite banks of a river, named Avene. The battle began, and was continued for some time with missiles; at length Offa with the bravest of his warriors crossed the stream, was followed by the main body of his army, put his enemies to flight, and pursued them with great slaughter. They rallied however, and renewed the fight with such obstinacy, that it was very doubtful what the result would be, when both parties, weary of the contest, were compelled to take rest. During the armistice, the insolence of two sons of Aliel, Hildebrand (or Brutus) and Sueno, provoked the vengeance of Offa, and they fell by his hand. The conflict was renewed, but victory soon declared for Offa; his enemies fled before him, Aliel was drowned in attempting to cross a stream, named after him Riganburn, and Mitun also fell. Offa gave honourable burial to the corpses of the nobles, who had fallen in the battle; and those of the rest of the slain were buried, under an immense heap of stones, which received in consequence the name of Qualmhul, (Slaughter-hill). The battle-field was called afterwards Blodewald.

The victory is thus noticed in the Traveller's Tale:—

" Offa ruled Ongle; Alewih, who was the proudest of
" those men, the Danes; yet did he not gain lordship over
" Offa, but Offa won, first of men, whilst yet a knight,
" most kingdoms. None of equal age with him, gained
" greater lordship in war. By his single sword he enlarged
" the march for the With-Myrgings, by Fifeld-ore. Angles
" and Swæfs held it thenceforth, as Offa won it."[1]

This passage, as far as it goes, agrees exactly with the S. Albans' tradition. Aliel is a corruption of Alewih; Rigan perhaps indicates the particular tribe to which he belonged, the Rugas, for these would be comprehended under the name of Danes; and Mitun is possibly a corruption of Witta, whom the Traveller mentions as having ruled the Swæfs.[2] The phrase *cniht wesende*, " whilst yet a knight," means, what the story tells us, that Offa had not attained to the royal dignity to which his birth entitled him, at the time of the battle.

The two accounts enable us to identify beyond a doubt

---

[1] L. 71-90. [2] L. 45.

the scene of this celebrated conflict. The Traveller says it was *bi Fifeld-ore*, which I translate " the beginning (or bor-" der) of Fifield;" and this is Fifield in Oxfordshire, separated from Gloucestershire by the river Evenlode, which I take to be the Avene of the story, the river on the banks of which the rival armies met. It is not of course to be expected that we should be able to find all the ancient names of places still in use; for a very large proportion of those which are mentioned in the Codex Diplomaticus cannot now be traced.[3] So we do not find Blodewald, doubtless *Bleddan-weald*, " the " wold of Bledda;"[4] but although his name has disappeared from the neighbouring wold, it still remains at Bledington,[5] the parish in Gloucestershire which borders on Fifield, and is separated from it by the Evenlode.

The names of the parishes of Swell and Slaughter supply a remarkable verification of the identity of this district with the scene of the battle. We are told that the corpses of the lower ranks of the slain were buried under a heap of stones,

---

[3] Salmonnesburg (137), which is known to have been in the neighbouring hundred of Slaughter, and indeed gave name to it, may be cited as an instance of such a name now lost.

[4] A chieftain, after whom Bleadon in Oxfordshire, and Bledlow (Bleddan hlæw) in Buckinghamshire, have been named.

[5] Bleddan-dún, as Seckington in Warwickshire was Seccandún, and Abingdon in Berkshire, Abbandún. It is not unusual to find that places, which once bore the names of chieftains, now bear those of his descendants. Thus Coludesburg in Berwickshire is now Coldingham. We also frequently find the name of the family and of its founder in close proximity, as in the instances of Shenlow in the parish of Shenington in Oxfordshire, Winterton and Wintringham in Lincolnshire, Repton in Derbyshire and Repington in Warwickshire. It is not improbable that the wold, north-west of Bledington, may have been called Bleddan-weald, the Blodewald of the story; the author of which may have altered the name in accordance with his own idea of its derivation.

which was called from the circumstance *Qualmhul,* " the hill
" of Slaughter." Slaughter-hill is doubtless the place indicated; it is three miles west of Bledington, and has given name to two neighbouring parishes, as well as to the hundred. The bodies of the nobles were buried apart; they would of course be burned, in accordance with the customs of the Teutonic tribes, (as exemplified in the cases of Hnæf and Beowulf); and although the story does not give the name of the place where this was done, the occurrence of the names of two villages, Upper and Lower Swell, in the immediate neighbourhood of the Slaughters, helps us to determine it. *Swell* certainly means " burning," or a " funeral pile;" the only other place in England which bears this name, is in Somersetshire, in the neighbourhood of another battle-field, that of Langport; and the Rev. David Royce, Vicar of Lower Swell, (to whom I am indebted for much interesting information relative to this group of parishes), tells me that a long deep bed of ashes was discovered in his churchyard, on digging foundations for the enlargement of the church; and that, of eleven barrows in the parish, the largest is called Picked Morden, a name which seems equivalent to " selected " slain." If this be correct, it will be that in which the burnt corpses of the nobles were buried. The field in which it stands is called Camp ground, and he says, that an old woman once told him, that the last battle that was fought in England was fought there. A well in the parish of Slaughter is called the king's well, where they say the king washed his wounds after the battle. A valley to the northward of these parishes is called the Danes' Beat.

The poem tells us that the result of the battle was the extension of the dominions of Offa, and the settlement of the boundary line between the Angles and the Swæfs; the story indicates that it was the addition of Gloucestershire to Wærmund's dominions; for it tells us that they were in Warwickshire, (in which county and in Worcestershire we have already noticed several traces of his name), and, four years after the battle, we are informed, that he was buried at Gloucester; and, in perfect accordance with the poem and the story at once, the county map shows us the Evenlode the boundary, for several miles, between Gloucestershire and Oxfordshire; " the march continues" to this day "as Offa won it, by " Fifeld-ore." The contest was not, however, confined to this neighbourhood; we are told of a flight and a pursuit, of a second battle, of the final discomfiture and flight of Offa's foes, and of their leader perishing in the Riganburn. This seems to be the Rugganbróc,[6] a stream which falls into the Stour, not far from its junction with the Avon. Battle bridges, near Chipping Campden, nearly in the direct line between Fifield and the Rugganbróc, is said to be so named from a battle fought there between the Mercians and West Saxons; and as none of the recorded battles, between these nations, appear to have been fought in this locality, it is probably Offa's conflict with Alewih of which this tradition speaks.

The names of Alewih and Witta occur at Alvescott and Witney, in Oxfordshire, about eight miles to the south-east of Fifield; that of the former at Alveston in Gloucestershire, and Alveston in Warwickshire; and this last is almost directly north of the junction of the stream, in which he is said to have perished, with the Stour; so that it would seem to indicate, that the object of his flight was to gain a fortress which belonged to him.

---

[6] Cod. Diplom. 55.

After the battle, Wærmund invested Offa with the royal dignity, and resigned the government of the kingdom into his hands. He died four years afterwards, at a very advanced age, and was buried at Gloucester. Offa enjoyed a prosperous reign, overcame all his enemies, and was enabled to hold his dominions for a long time in peace, whilst other kings were involved in war.

Some time afterwards, (as Matthew Paris relates), being separated from his retinue whilst hunting, he found a young girl, who said that she was the daughter of a prince of York, who had commanded her to be conveyed to that solitude and murdered, because she refused to submit to his lust, but that the executioners had spared her life, and left her there. Ross here supplies an important variation, viz. that, under the same circumstances, the maiden fled from her father, under the guidance of a faithful thane. Offa brought her home, and committed her to the care of his domestics; and, some years later, being importuned by his nobles to marry, took her to wife, and had children by her. Offa's wisdom and power were so widely celebrated, that other kings frequently sought his advice and assistance. An invasion of the Picts and Scots, on one occasion, compelled the King of Northumbria to ask him for aid; he offered him the supremacy of his kingdom, and requested the hand of his daughter in marriage without dowry, (to which an alliance with her father seems to have been considered equivalent). Offa accordingly led an army to assist him, obtained an easy victory over the enemy, and drove them back into Scotland. Whilst he was still in the North, he sent a messenger home with despatches. The messenger inadvertently stayed at the court of the father of Offa's queen, who contrived to intoxicate him, and to substitute for the despatches others, in which the regents of Offa's kingdom were commanded to have her conducted with her children to a lonely place, and mutilated, on the pretext that she was a sorceress. Although astonished at the receipt of such an order, they dared not disobey; the family were conveyed to a wilderness, where the children were slain, but the beauty of the mother moved the executioners to spare her; and a hermit, who lived in the neighbourhood, found them, obtained by his prayers the restoration of the children to life, and took care of them. Not long after his return home, Offa discovered the place of their retreat; the hermit urged him to found a monastery in thanksgiving, and he promised to do so, but died without having fulfilled his promise. It was fulfilled however by his descendant Winfrith, who, on account of the similarity of the circumstances of his own early life to those of his ancestor, assumed the name of Offa.

In the poem of Beowulf we have an allusion to some of the circumstances of this story, with the information that the lady whom Offa espoused, was also, and (as it seems) afterwards, the wife of Hygelac :—

"Although she was not mean, nor too sparing of gifts, of
" hoarded treasures, to the people of the Geats, Hæreth's
" daughter, the bold queen of the people, practised violence
" of mood, terrible wickedness. Save her wedded lord, who
" gazed on her every day with his eyes, none of the dear
" companions durst approach that beast, but she allotted, told
" to him, bands of slaughter, twisted with hands. Soon
" afterwards, after the grasp of hands, it was settled with the
" knife; so that the good sword must determine it, make
" known the fatal evil. Such is no queenly custom, for a
" lady to practise, though she be beautiful, that a peace-

"weaver should pursue a dear man for his life, for fierce
"anger. Heming's kinsman, at least, drinking ale, reviled
"her for that. Others said, that she had less perpetrated
"mighty evils, crafty malice, after she first was given adorned
"with gold to the young champion, the noble beast; after
"she sought Offa's court, in a journey over the fallow flood,
"by her father's command; where she afterwards, living
"well on the throne, in good repute, enjoyed life's creations,
"held high love with the prince of heroes, the best of noble
"race, of all mankind, between the seas, to my knowledge.
"For Offa, the spear-bold man, was widely renowned for
"gifts and wars. In wisdom he held his patrimony. From
"him Geomer sprang, for help to heroes, Heming's kinsman,
"Garmund's nephew, mighty in conflicts."[7]

As, then, Hygelac fell in battle, in or about A. D. 511, and his son Heardred was not then old enough to take the kingdom into his own hands, the death of Offa may be supposed to have occurred about the beginning of the sixth century.

The S. Albans' story differs from that in the poem, as to the circumstances under which this lady made her appearance in Offa's dominions; and whilst we are bound to follow the latter as the older and more trustworthy authority, it is not difficult to discover the clue to the principal variations in the former. The S. Albans' legend, for instance, says that her father was a prince of York, the poem that she came to Offa's court over "the fallow flood." It also appears that she was Hæreth's daughter, and Hereric's sister, (since Heardred was Hereric's nephew). Chararic, whom I have conjecturally identified with Hereric, reigned in the north-eastern provinces

---

[7] F. 172, 173.

of Gaul, and the name of Evreux, (Eburovices or Ebroicas) is so similar to that of York, (Eburacum, Ebraice, or Eferwic), that it is easy to understand, how Matthew Paris, compiling his life of Offa from the pictured history and from tradition, might mistake one for the other; and, having done this, it would be quite natural for him to place the territory of the king whom Offa went to assist, in Northumbria, and to call his enemies Picts and Scots.

Offa appears to have reigned over an extensive territory, and to have enjoyed a high reputation for wisdom and valour; it is not therefore incredible, (especially when we take into consideration the circumstances of the history of Arthur, and of Hygelac, his cotemporaries, and of the Anglian princess who compelled the king of the Varni, by force of arms, to marry her), that his aid, and the hand of his daughter in marriage, should have been sought by a continental sovereign; so that the sequel of the S. Albans' story may be substantially true.

Quite incidental, and yet very remarkable, is the coincidence between the story and the poem, in those passages which speak of the character of the queen. The poet gives two opposite characters of her, both from hearsay, and in such a way as to show that her memory was still fresh in men's minds, and her conduct freely discussed over their cups, when he composed his poem; the first, that she was a cruel sorceress, and this on the word of Heming's kinsman; the other, that she was a good queen, and an affectionate wife to Offa, and this on the authority of others, who said that she had not been guilty of the cruel practices attributed to her, at least since her union with him. In this latter character the poet himself represents her as the wife of Hygelac, saying:—

"Hæreth's daughter went through the hall with mead-servings, loved the people, bare the liquor-cup to the nobles to hand."[8]

Thus he bears witness to the general truth of the S. Albans' legend, which also indicates that she had both these characters; one which her father imputed to her, (perhaps in palliation of his conduct towards her), and one which she really maintained in the kingdom in which she found refuge; for the reason assigned for the cruel orders, given in the despatches which her father is said to have substituted for those of Offa, was that she was a sorceress, the character with which Heming's kinsman reproached her.

This difference also satisfactorily accounts for the discrepancy between the story and the poem, with regard to the circumstances under which she sought refuge in Offa's kingdom. Her father would represent her flight as a banishment on account of her crimes, whereas the truth probably was, as Ross relates it, that she fled to escape from him, under the guidance of a trusty thane.

Thus, whilst the S. Albans' story furnishes an important complement to the brief notices of Offa in Beowulf and the Traveller's Tale, its variations from them are accounted for, by the supposition of a mistake, (into which Matthew Paris might easily fall), with regard to the name of the city where the father of Offa's queen reigned, and by the peculiar circumstances of her history. The community of S. Albans may well have possessed, from early times, documents relative to the history of their founder's ancestor, which had a particular interest for them, inasmuch as it is said, that the founda-

[8] F. 173.

tion of their house by Offa II. was an obligation contracted by Offa I, and bequeathed to his son. Nor have we any right to call in question the circumstance, which is implied, of the first Offa having been a Christian. So far from being incredible, it is perfectly consistent with statements which we find elsewhere, relative to the history of these times,—notices of Saxons having embraced Christianity, and, as Christians, having been allowed to retain their settlements undisturbed, when their Pagan kindred were expelled from the island. Many conversions to Christianity may have occurred, whilst the British bishops still retained possession of their sees, and great numbers of clergy still remained in Britain. It was during this period, anterior to Garmund's exterminating persecution, that Offa reigned. If, as is probable, he kept aloof from the conflicts which the Northumbrians waged with Arthur during the years 467 to 471, and the struggle which Cerdic maintained with him a few years afterwards, he would be allowed to hold his kingdom in peace, (as it is stated that he did, whilst other kings were involved in war), unmolested by Arthur, whose wars with the Saxons were rather defensive than offensive. His being a Christian, if such were indeed the case, would contribute to the maintainance of this peace between them; but whether he was a Christian or not, the author of Beowulf, the Traveller, and the Monk of S. Albans, unanimously accord to him the character of a brave and successful warrior, and a wise and good king.

CHAPTER VI.

The Story of Horn.

HIS story, once very popular with our forefathers, as Chaucer and Lydgate testify, properly claims a place here; because, although it is not preserved in anything like the ancient form in which that of Hygelac and Beowulf comes to us, and therefore cannot be considered of equal authority, it speaks of events of the same age, and throws some light on an obscure passage, which refers to the history of Beowulf's father. It is presented to us:—

    I. In a very good English version of the fourteenth century;[1] defective at the end.

    II. In a French version of the twelfth;[2] complete.

    III. In another English version of the fourteenth;[3] defective at the beginning and end.

The first, as Mr. Coneybeare has justly remarked, bears the clearest marks of having been derived from an early Anglo-Saxon original; and the fact, that it gives pure An-

---

[1] Advocates' Library, Edinburgh, W. 4, 1. (Ritson's Metrical Romances, vol. III. 282).

[2] Harleian MS. 527.   [3] Ibid. 2253.

glo-Saxon names to the English, and Celtic names to the
Welsh and Irish personages, whom it mentions, affords a
presumption of its general truthfulness. In the general outlines of the story, the other two agree with this, although
they differ in the details; but the names in the second agree
more nearly with those in the first, than do those in the
third. The last indeed seems to be the composition of a
minstrel, who was very imperfectly acquainted with the story,
and filled up the meagre outlines which his memory retained,
with names and circumstances of his own devising. I shall
take the story, therefore, as it is in the first, borrowing an
occasional illustration from the others.

A prince, whose name was doubtless Heatholaf,[4] appears
to have reigned in Yorkshire, where Haddlesley, in the parish
of Birkin, preserves the only trace of this name that can be
found in this country. By his queen, Godild, he had a son
named Horn, whom he placed under the tutorship of his
steward Herlaund, along with eight youths, sons of his
thanes,—Hatherof, Tebaude, Athelstan, Winwold, Gariis,
Wihard, Witard,[5] and Wikel,—whom he had chosen for his
son's companions.

A Danish fleet entered the Tees, and their crews disembarked in Cleveland; but Heatholaf promptly assembled his
forces on Northallerton moor, attacked, and defeated them.
He then went to hunt on Blackmoor, (near Helmsley), and
afterwards held a feast at Pickering. Thence he went to

---

[4] Hatheolf, I. Aoluf, II. Allof, III. In I. he is said to have reigned
north of the Humber, in II. his dominions are said to have been in
"Bretaine," in III. they are generally called "Suddene," *i. e.* "Suth-
"Denas."

[5] Or Wigard.

York, where, after exacting from his son's young companions an oath of fidelity to him, he gave to them the lands which their fathers, who had fallen in the battle, had held of himself. Nine months after this victory, three kings,—Ferwele, Winwald and Malkan,—came from Ireland, and invaded Westmoreland. Heatholaf again collected his forces, and gave them battle on Stainmoor. Ferwele and Winwald, and nearly the whole of each army perished; and Heatholaf, maimed by the stones which the remnant of his foes cast upon him, was despatched by Malkan, who then returned to Ireland.

In the French version, his death is ascribed, in one place to Romuld, (who from the epithet bestowed upon him, "le "malfé," would seem to have been a traitor and rebel), in another to Rollac, son of Godebrand, and nephew of Herebrant and Hildebrant. This remarkable variation in the French MS., (not necessarily a contradiction, since several persons appear to have had a part in Heatholaf's death), enables us to identify Heatholaf with the prince whose fall is alluded to in Beowulf; for here we have the names of three brothers Godebrand, Herebrand, and Hildibrand; and Herebrand with his son, a second Hildibrand, and his grandson, Heathobrand, are the famous Wylfings of the sagas.

Beowulf's father was Ecgtheow, a Wægmunding, "to "whom Hrethel of the Geats gave his only daughter in "marriage,"[6] and as it said that he was "known to nations, "well remembered throughout the earth,"[7] it is probable that he played a conspicuous part in the wars of his time. Hrothgar is represented saying to Beowulf, on his arrival at his court :—

---

[6] F. 138. [7] F. 135.

" Thy father quelled his greatest enemy. With the Wyl-
" fings he slew Heatholaf, when the spear-folk could not
" overcome him, for dread of his prowess. Thence, over the
" rolling of the waves, he sought the South-Danes' folk, the
" favour of the Scyldings; when I indeed ruled the Danes'
" folk, and held in my youth wide realms, the treasure city
" of heroes."—" Afterwards I settled that feud with money.
" I sent old treasures to the Wylfings over the water's back.
" He swore oaths to me."[8]

Now if we compare this passage with the stanzas in the poem,[9] which describe the battle, and the death of Heatholaf,

---

[8] F. 140.

[9]
" The Irise ost was long and brade,
" On Stainesmore ther thai rade,
  " Thai yaf a crie for pride;
" Hende Hatheolf hem abade,
" Swiche meting was never made,
  " With sorwe on ich a side.
" Right in a litel stounde,
" Sexti thousand wer layd to grounde,
  " In herd is nought to hide;
" King Hathcolf slough with his hond,
" That was comen out of Yrlond,
  " Two kinges that tide.

" King Hatheolf was wel wo,
" For the Irise ost was mani and mo,
  " With scheld and with spere;
" Ful long seththen man said so,
" When men schuld to batayl go,
  " To men might on dere.
" Thei King Hatheolf saught fast;
" King Malkan stiked attélast,
  " His stede that schuld him bere.
" Now schal men finde kinges fewe,
" That in batayl be so trewe,
  " His lond for to were.

we find in the latter a satisfactory explanation of one at least of the obscure allusions in the former. We are told that, after Malkan had killed Heatholaf's horse and forced him to fight on foot, the Irish folk pressed upon him, intending either to kill or capture him; that he defended himself so bravely, that they were forced to keep at a distance, until, by hurling stones at him, they had completely disabled him; and that Malkan then thrust his sword into his heart. Ecgtheow and the Wylfings,[10] and perhaps Romuld also, might be engaged

> " When King Hatheolf on fot strode,
> " The Yrise folk about him yode,
>   " As hondes do to bare.
> " Whom he hit opon the hode,
> " Were he never knight so gode,
>   " He yave a dint wel sare;
> " He brought in a litel stounde,
> " Wel fif thousende to grounde,
>   " With his grimly gare.
> " The Yrise ost tok hem to red,
> " To ston that douhti knight to ded,
>   " Thai durst neighe him na mare.
>
> " Gret diol it was to se,
> " Of hende Hatheolf that was so fre,
>   " Stones to him thai cast,
> " Thai brak him bothe legge and kne,
> " Gret diol it was to se,
>   " He kneled attelast;
> " King Malcan with wretthe out stert,
> " And smote King Hatheolf to the hert,
>   " He held his wepen so fast,
> " That King Malcan smot his arm atwo,
> " Ere he might gete his swerd him fro,
>   " For nede his hert to brast."

[10] We have a remarkable verification of the fact of the Wylfings having been connected with the history of Northumbria, and associated with the Irish, in the occurrence of the name of Herebrand at Herebrandston in

in this affair; for, by the Anglo-Saxon name, which the English poem gives to one of the three kings who came from Ireland, it implies that a part of the invading army was Anglo-Saxon; and so far coincides with the French version, which represents Herebrand and Hildibrand as going to Ireland some years later, and opposed to Horn, in the battle in which Malkan fell.

The names of the other kings, who were opposed to Heatholaf, are purely Celtic. Ferwele, (identical with Fernwail or Farinmagil), occurs at least three times in history,—as borne by the son of Idwal, the king who fell at Dirham, and a descendant of Vortigern; and Malkan, (the same as Mailcun, Maglocun, or Maelgwn), was the name of two princes at least, who figure in the history of the fifth and sixth centuries.

The battle must have been fought early in the second half of the fifth century, for it was during Hrothgar's youth. It was, therefore, before Ecgtheow and Hrethel left Yorkshire and went to Suffolk; for Ecgtheow and the Wylfings must have been neighbours to Heatholaf, if it was necessary for the weregild to be paid, before the feud could be settled. The treasures which Hrothgar sent, enabled the Wylfings to do this, and as it was some time afterwards, it was probably after Horn's return to his paternal dominions.

On the death of Heatholaf, an earl of Northumberland seized upon his territory. His name appears from the French version to have been Romund, possibly Hrothmund of the

---

Pembrokeshire, amongst a number of English names, which seems to be most satisfactorily accounted for, by the circumstance of that district having been the scene of an invasion of Scots from Ireland, and Angles from Northumbria in A.D. 449.

East-Anglian genealogy, whose name occurs at Romanby[11] near Northallerton.

Herlaund fled with his youthful charge to the court of King Houlak,[12] "fer southe in Inglond," who received them graciously and promised them his protection. His territory must have been in East Anglia, for it was far to the southward of Heatholaf's kingdom, Horn came to it by sea, and, when banished from it, made a long journey westward into Wales. Lions, therefore, which the French version gives as the name of his residence, may indicate King's Lynn, and so Houlak may have reigned in the district, which, up to the time of Hencgest's expedition, not long before, had been occupied by Finn.

Houlak had no son by his queen, but a daughter, Riminild. She became enamoured of Horn, and gave him for his knightly outfit, a horse, a horn, and a sword of Weland's workmanship. Horn and Hatherof were then knighted by the king; Tebaud and Winwald crossed the sea, and took service with the king of France; Gariis and Athelston, in like manner, joined the retinue of an earl in Bretaigne; and the rest remained with Houlak. Wigard and Wikel traduced Horn and Riminild to her father, and Horn was banished from his court. He assumed the name of Godebounde,[13] and journeyed westward into Wales, where he entered into the service of Elidan, a king who dwelt on Snowdon.

Elidan, of course, is a British name. It was borne by a Bishop of Alclud, mentioned by Geoffrey as promoted to that

---

[11] Romundebi, Domesday.
[12] Hunlaf, who reigned in Bretaigne at Lyons, II.
[13] Gudmod, II. Godmod, III.

see by Arthur. No other of the name appears to be mentioned in history, but it is possible that Elidan here may be a contraction of Elidyr Lydanwyn,[14] the name of Llywarch Hên's father, a prince who certainly lived in the fifth century, but of whom nothing more is known.

Whilst Horn was with him, messengers came from Finlak, a king of Ireland, entreating aid against Malkan. Horn was sent thither, and landed at Yolkil. A battle ensued, in which he killed Malkan, and recovered his father's sword, but was himself severely wounded.[15]

Yolkil may be either Dalkey, the nearest point on the Irish coast to Wales, or Youghal. Finlak is Findloga, a name which was borne by two Irish princes who lived in the fifth century. One was the father of S. Finnian of Clonard,[16] the other of S. Brendan of Clonfert.[17] The former was more probably the king to whose assistance Horn was sent.

Finlak gave to Horn the territory of Malkan, and wished to have given him his daughter in marriage, but Horn would not

---

[14] For this suggestion I am indebted to Mr. Stephens of Merthyr-Tydfyl.

[15] In the French version it is said that Hildibrant and Herebrant arrived in Ireland, and sent their nephew Rollac to demand tribute of the king, (who is called Gudred); that Horn fought with and slew him; that Hydebrant killed the king's sons; and that their death was avenged by Horn.

[16] Who in the hymn for his feast is said to have been—

" Nativus de Lageniâ
" Qui nomen sprevit regium."

The Annals of the Four Masters record his death A.D. 548, and the editor in a note refers to O'Clery's Irish Calendar, where he is mentioned as the son of Finnlogh, son of Fintan of the Clanna Rudhraighe, and it is said that he died A.D. 552, or according to others in A.D. 563.

[17] He was born in A.D. 484 in Kerry.

forsake his troth, plighted to Riminild. Intelligence reached him that a king named Moging[18] was a suitor for her hand at Houlak's court, and he returned at once to prevent the marriage. Having defeated his enemies, and justified himself with the king, he espoused Riminild, and then led an expedition into Northumbria, to recover his father's kingdom.

Here the MS. abruptly breaks off, with the mention of Thorbrand, who would seem to have been a prince in Northumbria; and Horn's subsequent history is lost.[19]

The territory of Moging was probably in Derbyshire, for his name and that of Reynis occur in that county, at Muggington[20] and Renishaw, but nowhere else in England.

---

[18] Modun of Fenice, II. Mody of Reynis, III.
[19] III. merely says that his expedition was successful, and that he reigned with Riminild in Northumbria.
[20] Mogintone, Domesday.

CHAPTER VII.

The Story of Beowulf; the Accession of Ælle in Deira; the Arrival of Ida; and the Chronology of the Reigns of his Successors.

ROTHGAR says of Beowulf, "I knew him "when he was a cniht;"[1] that is, before he attained to the princely rank, to which his birth entitled him, whilst he was at the court of Hrethel; for Beowulf says of himself:—

" I was seven winters old, when the prince of treasures,
" the lordly friend of peoples, King Hrethel, took me from
" my father, held and had me, gave me treasure and feast,
" remembered our kinship; I was a prince in his dwellings,
" not in any wise less dear to him in life, than any one of his
" children, Herebeald, and Hæthcyn, or my Hygelac."[2]

Hrothgar's acquaintance with him must have been whilst this family were his neighbours, before they settled in Suffolk.

Among the exploits of Beowulf's youth, particular mention is made of a rowing-match, (for so it seems to me it must be understood), with Brecca prince of the Brondings, in which

---

[1] F. 138. [2] F. 184.

Beowulf was victor. He is said to have reached the shore of *Finna land*, the " land of the Fins," and Brecca to have landed " at Heatho-Ræmis, whence he, beloved by his people, " sought his dear territory, the land of the Brondings, his " fair peaceful burgh, where he owned a people, a burgh, " and rings."[3]

Beowulf and Brecca, therefore, were neighbours; Brecca's principality was not far from Hrethel's court. Heatho-Ræmis must be on the coast, and the territory of the Brondings at some distance inland. The former I take to be Ramsey in Essex, or Ramsholt in Suffolk, which is not far from it. About ten miles from Rattlesden is Breckley, bearing the name of Brecca; and Bransfield, Brandeston, Brantham, and Brandon, in the same county, may indicate settlements of the Brondings, as they seem to be named after their father Brand or Brond. Of the Fins there is now no trace on the coast, but two Finboroughs, not far from Rattlesden, show that they were settled in this district, neighbours, if not subjects, of Hrethel.

Beowulf was with Hygelac in his campaign against the Sweos, for he says of him, immediately after his notice of it:—

" I repaid in war, as it was granted to me, with my shining " sword, the treasures which he gave to me. He granted " me land the joy of a patrimony. He had no need to seek, " buy with value, worse warriors among the Gifthas, nor " among the Gar-Danes, nor in Sweo-rice. Thus I in con-" flict, alone in the array, would do battle before him."[4]

Some time after this, during Hygelac's reign, he resolved to go to Heort, for the purpose of combating the giant Grendel, of whose cruelty tidings had reached him.

---

[3] F. 141. [4] F. 185.

"He commanded to make ready for him a good wave-traverser, said he would seek the war-king, the great prince, over the swan-road, since he had need of men.—— The good chief had chosen champions of the Geat's people, of those whom he might find the keenest. With fifteen he sought the sea-wood; a warrior, a water-crafty man, pointed out the land-boundaries. The time passed on. The floater was on the waves, the boat under the hill, the warriors ready stepped on the prow, the streams rolled, the sea against the sand. The warriors bare bright ornaments, beautiful war-gear, into the bosom of the bark. The men shoved out the bounden wood on the welcome voyage. Then, most like to a bird, the foam-necked floater, wafted by the wind, departed over the wave-sea, until that the wreathed prow had sailed about one-hour of another day, so that the voyagers saw land sea-cliffs shine, steep mountains, wide sea-nesses. Then was the sea traversed, at the end of their toil."[5]

The Scyldings' coast-guard rode down to the shore to meet them, and having learned from them that they were come to offer their assistance to Hrothgar, committed their vessel to the care of his brother officers, conducted them until they came within sight of Heort, and then returned to his post. Arrived at the palace, they were challenged by one of Hrothgar's thanes, and then Wulfgar, prince of the Wendels, undertook to report their coming to the king. They were ushered into his presence, graciously received, and entertained at a feast. The following night, Beowulf vanquished the giant; two days afterwards he slew Grendel's

---

[5] F. 134.

mother; and then, loaded with presents by Hrothgar and Wealhtheow, embarked on his homeward voyage.

"He departed in the vessel, stirring the deep water, left
"the land of the Danes. There was by the mast a sea-
"mantle, a sail cord-fast; the sea-wood groaned, nor there
"did the wind, over the billows, hinder the wave-floater
"from its journey. The sea-goer went, the foam-necked
"floated forth over the wave, the bounden prow over the
"ocean streams, so that they might descry the Geat's cliffs,
"the known nesses. The keel sprang up, forced by the
"wind, stood on land. Quickly at the sea the shore-guard
"was ready, who a long time before had watched the course
"of the dear men, ready at the shore. He secured the wide-
"bosomed ship, fast with anchor-bonds to the sand, lest the
"force of the waves might wreck it, the winsome wood. He
"commanded then to bear up the treasure of the æthelings,
"the ornament, and solid gold. They had not thence far to
"seek the giver of treasure, Hygelac the Hrethling, where
"he dwelleth at home with his comrades near the sea-wall.
"The building was excellent, the king a famous prince; the
"hall high, Hygd very young, wise, well-established, though
"he had dwelt few winters within the burgh-enclosure."[6]

From these two descriptions, of Beowulf's outward and homeward voyage, it appears that he started from and arrived at the same point; but, whereas at starting he had some distance to travel before he reached the sea, on his return he found Hygelac resident near the shore. This residence was perhaps Uggeshall, and the point of embarkation some place on the neighbouring coast. Covehithe is the nearest point

---

[6] F. 171, 172.

to Uggeshall; its name indicates an ancient harbour, and it answers the description in the poem very well. Hence to Hartlepool the distance may be computed at about two hundred and twenty miles, a distance which might well be accomplished in the time specified, from an early hour in the morning of one day until one o'clock of the next, with a fair wind.[7] On the outward voyage, as they drew near to land, the lofty cliffs of the Yorkshire coast would present themselves to their view, and then the cliffs of Hartlepool, on which Hrothgar's coast-guard was stationed; and after passing the latter, they would disembark on the sands to the north, whence a journey of about two miles would bring them to Hart. On their homeward voyage they descried the well-known cliffs of the Geats, the high lands between Lowestoft and Southwold.

After his return, Beowulf was associated in the kingdom with Hygelac, who—

"Gave him seven thousand, a dwelling and throne. The
"land was natural to them both together in the nation; the
"territory, the patrimonial right stronger in the other, the
"wide realm his who there was the better."[8]

As we have already noticed, it is intimated that he led an expedition to the assistance of Hrothgar against the Heatho-Beards. He was the companion of Hygelac in every enter-

---

[7] I am not aware that we have any data, whereon to found a judgment as to the speed of the vessels in use amongst our forefathers. It seems probable that they are fairly represented as to form by the primitive cobles of the fishermen of the Yorkshire coast; and, (as they were constructed for quick sailing, by a people who paid great attention to navigation), not unreasonable to suppose that their speed was equal to that of these cobles, *i.e.* about eight miles an hour.

[8] F. 178.

prise, and in the last fatal expedition, which cost the king his life, his valour was particularly distinguished:—

"I, for valour, was the handslayer of Dæghræfn, the champion of the Hugas. He might by no means bring the treasure, the breast-ornament, to the Frisian king, but he, the keeper of the standard, the ætheling, fell in battle. Nor was the sword his bane, but I grasped in conflict the flowings of his heart, I brake the bone-house."[9]

The poet also follows up his notice of the fall of Hygelac, with a special remembrance of the part which his hero played in the enterprise:—

"Thence Beowulf came by his own valour. He bore a separate part.[10] He had on his arm —— thirty war-suits, when he went down to the sea. The Hetwaras, active in war, who before bare the shield against him, had no need of boasting. Few returned from the war-bold man, to visit their home. Then he the son of Ecgtheow, a poor solitary, swam[11] over the path of seals, back to his people, where Hygd had given him treasury and kingdom, rings and a throne. He trusted not in his son that he could hold his paternal seats against foreign people. Then was Hygelac dead."[12]

This passage supplies information, additional to that in the last chapter, relative to this expedition, victorious at first, unfortunate in its result. It would seem that Hygelac and

---

[9] F. 185.

[10] So I translate "sund-nytte dreáh."

[11] The word *swimman* appears to be used, here and elsewhere, in the sense of to "traverse the sea." We know, from the French accounts, that this was a naval expedition; so, of course, Beowulf had a ship in which to return.

[12] F. 182.

Beowulf, in their invasion of the Hetwaras' country, divided their forces, and ravaged it in different directions; and that Beowulf returned from his foray with the spoils of thirty foes, whom he had slain. He is said to have returned solitary, because he had lost in Hygelac, his uncle, his partner in the kingdom, and his dearest friend.

We give the sequel of his history in the poet's own words.

" Not the sooner for that might the poor people find, at
" the hands of the ætheling, on any account, that he would
" be lord to Heardred, or would choose the kingdom. But
" he supported him among the people with friendly counsels,
" with honour joyfully, until he grew older; he ruled the
" Weder-Geats."[13]

" So the son of Ecgtheow, a man known for wars, grew
" old in good deeds, he acted after judgment, nor did he
" drunkenly strike his hearth-enjoyers. His soul was not
" cruel."[14]

He seems however to have incurred the dislike of his people for a time, on account of this disinterested affection for his young cousin, and his reluctance to engage in aggressive wars:—

" Long was the shame, that the sons of the Geats, on the
" mead-bench, did not reckon him good, nor would make him
" of much account, the lord of their hosts. Very oft they
" said that he was lazy, a base ætheling. A reverse of every
" grievance came to the glorious man."[15]

By the death of Heardred, who fell in a battle with the Scylfings, of which two passages in the poem speak some-

---

[13] F. 182. [14] F. 178. [15] Ibid.

what obscurely, he was left in sole possession of the kingdom :—

"After Hygelac fell, and war-swords became the bane to
"Heardred, under the shield-wall, when hard war-bold men,
"the warlike Scylfings, sought him among the victorious
"people, overcame Hereric's nephew in wars, Beowulf after-
"wards received the broad kingdom into his hand; he held
"it well fifty winters. That was a good king, an old
"guardian of the land."[16]

"Avengers, the sons of Ohthere, sought him over the sea;
"they had deposed the helm of the Scylfings, the best of
"sea-kings, of those who distributed treasure in Swiorice,
"the great prince. That was for a token to him. He then,
"unsupported, the son of Hygelac, received a deadly wound
"with the swingings of the sword; and then, after Heardred
"fell, the son of Ongentheow returned to visit his home.
"Then he let Beowulf hold the throne, rule the Geats; that
"was a good king. He remembered retribution, for that
"ruin of the people, in later days. He became a friend to
"Eadgils, when distressed, supported him with people, over
"the wide sea. Afterwards he punished the son of Ohthere
"with warriors and weapons, with cold care-wanderings,
"deprived the king of life."[17]

From these passages we learn, that the sons of Ohthere had rebelled against Eadgils, Ongentheow's son, (doubtless by a former wife), driven him from his kingdom, and then pursued him to the country of Beowulf and Heardred, whither he had fled for refuge; that they were worsted in the battle which ensued, for, (although Heardred fell), Eadgils was enabled to

---

[16] F. 178, 179. [17] F. 182, 183.

return home; and that Beowulf assisted him with a fleet, and overcame and slew one of Ohthere's sons. This was Eanmund, who in another passage is said to have fallen by the hand of Weohstan, Beowulf's kinsman:—

"He drew his old sword, which was, among men, a relic
"of Eanmund, the son of Ohthere; of whom, when a friend-
"less wanderer, Weohstan was the slayer in conflict, with
"edges of the sword; and he bare away from his kinsman
"the brown-hued helmet, the ringed byrnie, the old Eotenish
"sword, which Onela had given him, his kinsman's battle-
"weeds, the ready furniture of war. He spake not of the
"feud, though he had exiled his brother's son."[18]

During the whole of Beowulf's reign, after Hygelac's fall, he is said to have been at feud with the Mere-Wioings:—

"Ever since, the Mere-Wioings' peace has been refused
"to us."[19]

In this name we may recognize the Wiwings, or people of Wiwa, whose name we have noticed at Wiveton in Norfolk, and who founded the kingdom of the East Angles early in the sixth century. Having recently arrived, and settled on the coast, they would be called Mere or Sea-Wioings; they would be Beowulf's neighbours; and the terms, in which this feud is mentioned, seem to imply that its result was disastrous to him. Here, then, we are enabled to connect the termination of Beowulf's rule in East Anglia, with the foundation of the historic kingdom of the East Angles; and we may presume that this feud was the occasion of his accepting the kingdom of the Scyldings, after the fall of Hrothgar's race. That he did so, appears from a speech of one of his thanes, who,—in

---

[18] F. 188. [19] F. 193.

continuation of his story, above cited, of the war between the Geats and Scylfings,—says:—

"That is the feud and enmity, the deadly malice of men, on account of which I expect that the Sweos' people will seek us, after they shall hear that our lord is dead; who before held treasure and kingdom against enemies, established folk-right after the fall of heroes, the bold Scyldings, or yet further practised valour."[20]

This is one of those prospective speeches, which the poet puts into the mouth of his heroes, alluding to events, of which he was cognizant as having occurred after the time of his story; and, as we have connected Beowulf's reign with the foundation of the East Anglia kingdom on the one hand, so, on the other, this speech is valuable, as assisting us to connect these events with the authentic history of Northumbria. For it is very probable that the invasion of Eoppa and Ida was the occasion of the fall of Hrothgar's race.

They arrived at Flamborough, with a fleet of sixty ships, during the first half of the sixth century, but their territory appears to have been beyond the Tyne; so that probably they were defeated in Deira, moved northward, and founded the kingdom of Bernicia, of which Ida became the sovereign in A.D. 547. The History of the Britons concludes with the following notice:[21]—

"The more the Saxons were vanquished in wars, the more

---

[20] F. 194.

[21] "Quanto magis vero Saxones prosternebantur in bellis, tanto magis a Germaniâ, et ab aliis augebantur Saxonibus; atque reges et duces cum multis militibus, ab omnibus pene provinciis ad se invitabant; et hoc egerunt usque ad tempus quo Ida regnavit, filius Eboba (Eobda, V.) Ipse primus rex fuit in Bernech, et in Cair Afrauc de genere Saxonum." C. 56.

"they were reinforced from Germany, and by other Saxons; and they invited to themselves kings and chiefs from almost all provinces with many warriors; and they did this until the time when Ida reigned, the son of Eobda. He was the first king in Berneich, and in Cair Affrauc, of the race of the Saxons."

Henry of Huntingdon says:[22]—

"When the chiefs of the Angles, in many and great battles, had conquered for themselves that country, they chose one Ida, a very noble youth, for their king. He reigned twelve years, always in arms and toils, and constructed Bebbanburgh, and surrounded it first with a hedge, and then with a wall. This kingdom began in the year of grace 547."

Allowing, therefore, some time for the reign of Eoppa, the arrival of these chieftains must have been some years previous. Foiled, I suppose, by Beowulf, who came to the aid of the Scyldings, and prevented from forming a settlement in the province in which they landed, they retired to the northward, established beyond the Tyne the kingdom of the Beornicas, (or descendants of Beornec), and fixed their residence at Bamborough. So the Cambrian genealogist also tells us:[23]—

"Ida, the son of Eobba, held the regions in the northern

---

[22] "Cum enim proceres Anglorum, multis et magnis præliis patriam (sc. Nordhumbrorum) sibi subjugassent, Idam quendam, juvenem nobilissimum, sibi regem constituerunt.—Hic igitur regnavit XII annis fortissime, semper armatus et laboriosus: construxit autem Bebanburgh, et circundedit eam prius sepe, postea muro. Regnum hoc incepit anno gratiæ DXLVII."

[23] "Ida, filius Eobba, tenuit regiones in sinistrali parte Britanniæ, id est, Umbri maris, et regnavit annis duodecim, et vixit Dinguayrth Guarth Berneich."

"part of Britain, that is, of the Umber sea, and reigned twelve years, and lived at Dinguayrth Guarth Berneich:"—

And how the name of the place was changed to Bebbanburch:—

"Eadlfered Flesaurs—gave to his wife, who is called Bebbab, Dinguoaroy (or Dinguayrdi), and it received its name, that is, Bebbanburch, from the name of his wife."[24]

This, doubtless, is the Cair Affrauc of the Paris and Vatican MSS. of the History of the Britons, (not noticed in the others), for Gaimar tells us, that Bamborough was founded by Ebrauc, and restored by Ida; so that even the evidence of these two MSS. does not contravene that of every other authority,—that Ida's kingdom was Bernicia only.

To return to our hero. Beowulf eventually reigned at Hart, where his early triumph over Grendel was gained; and in its neighbourhood the scenes of his last adventures are placed. We are told, that—

"The fire-dragon, the earth-warder, had utterly destroyed the fortress of the people, an island without."[25]

This, doubtless, indicates some convulsion of nature, and of such a convulsion the shore of Hartness presents undeniable traces. For a distance of nearly two miles south of the Slake of Hartlepool, between high and low water marks, the soil is filled with the remains of large trees, and heaps of agglomerated leaves, containing abundance of hazel-nuts; and the convulsion which submerged this forest may also have destroyed the island without, of which possibly the Longscar rock, immediately south of Hartlepool, may be the remnant.

---

[24] "Eadlfered Flesaur—dedit uxori suæ Dinguoaroy, quæ vocatur Bebbab, et de nomine uxoris suscepit nomen, id est, Bebbanburch."

[25] F. 181.

This was ascribed to the wrath of a dragon, whose hoard had been plundered; and the story of Beowulf's encounter with the monster follows. Its credibility must depend upon that of many others of the same kind, told of other heroes. It relates that Beowulf, knowing that a wooden shield would be of no use, provided himself with one of iron, and attacked the dragon with his sword, but could not inflict a wound, and was in danger of perishing, when a young warrior, his kinsman Wiglaf, came to his assistance. The wooden shield of the latter was destroyed at once by the dragon, so that he was compelled to fight by Beowulf's side, under the protection of his. Beowulf now struck the monster on the head, with no other result than the fracture of his sword, but Wiglaf contrived to plunge his into its body, and so brought the conflict to a close. The effects of the wound, which Beowulf had received in the first onset, began to appear; and in spite of the tender care of Wiglaf, who washed it, and sprinkled him with water, when fainting, he died shortly afterwards.

Now we may ask, if this story had been an invention, why should not Beowulf have been the victor, like Sigemund, and other heroes of these stories? Why should the poet have ascribed the honour of killing the monster, not to his hero, but to Wiglaf, who but for this adventure would not have been noticed at all? In this, as in another of these stories, the prowess of the hero would have been unavailing, but for assistance rendered at the critical moment. Are not these circumstances indications, that the story had at least some foundation in fact? Let it pass, however, for what it is worth, in the reader's judgment, when compared with others, (for which he is referred to the Appendix). The author, at least, believed it; there can be no doubt that he had in view the scene in which tradition placed the adventure, and that scene can even now be identified. It is described in several passages:—

"The mound all prepared, new by the cliff, stood in a "field, near to the water-waves."[26]

This passage speaks of its original construction, long before Beowulf's time, when it received the treasures, of which it was plundered by his thanes. The next speaks of it at the time, as—

"A mound under the earth, near to the holm-raging, the "strife of waves. Within, it was full of ornaments and "wires, a strong stone-hill; a path lay under, unknown to "men."[27]

"He saw there by the wall a stone arch stand, a stream "break out thence from the hill."[28]

"He looked on the giant's work, how the stone-arches, "fast on props, held the eternal earth-hall within."[29]

From these notices it is evident that it was a tumulus, containing chambers, formed of large flag-stones set on edge, supporting others laid horizontally over them;[30] and it was on a cliff, over which Beowulf's companions are said to have shoved the body of the dragon, and which was called Earna-næs. The scene was evidently well-known to the poet, and I have no hesitation in identifying it with Eagles-cliff, a promontory in Durham, about fifty feet high, nearly surrounded by the Tees.

Eagles-cliff is an exact translation of Earna-næs, and this name was doubtless given to it after the Conquest, when the Norman-French word *eagle* supplanted the Anglo-Saxon

---

[26] F. 179. [27] Ibid. [28] F. 186. [29] F. 189.
[30] Such as those at Uleybury in Gloucestershire, and New Grange near Drogheda.

earn,[31] and when the reason of its original name having been conferred upon it was forgotten; for Earndale, a few miles to the south-west, indicates a settlement of a tribe called Earnas in the neighbourhood; and possibly Yarm, on the south bank of the Tees, opposite Eagles-cliff, may be a contraction of Earna-ham. There is no tumulus now on Eagles-cliff; its materials would be too valuable to be spared, when stone was needed for the construction of the church and village which now occupy the promontory; but the spring still rises in the churchyard, and falls into the Tees. The river of course still retains its old Celtic name; that which is given to it in the poem being merely a generic name, bestowed by the Angles on other rivers as well.[32]

Beowulf's last instructions to Wiglaf, for his funeral, were:—

"Command the warlike brave, to make a mound at the sea-headland, bright after the funeral-pile, which shall rise high for a memorial to my people, on Hrónes-næs; that hereafter sea-farers may call it Beowulf's hill, when the Brentings drive afar over the darkness of the floods."[33]

Hron's name is preserved in that of Runswick village near Whitby; four miles to the north of which there is a lofty headland, which may well have been Hrónes-næs, for on it is the village of Boulby, the name of which is an easy contraction of Beowulfes-beorh. Beowulf's instructions indicate, that the Brentings were accustomed to make voyages past

---

[31] In the Anglo-Saxon vocabularies we find only *earn*; Layamon has *ærn*; in the fifteenth century the Norman French word had taken its place, for in vocabularies of that period we have *eggle*, *egylle*, and *egyle*.

[32] The Holme, for instance, in Yorkshire, a tributary of the Calder.

[33] F. 190, 191.

the headland chosen for his tomb; and accordingly we find a settlement of this tribe in Yorkshire, near the shore of the Humber, at Brantingham.

The reign of Beowulf over the Geats is said to have lasted fifty years. This period, computed from the time of his visit to Hrothgar's court, immediately after which he was raised to the throne by Hygelac, (some years before A.D. 511), brings the time of his death so near to the generally received date of the accession of Ælle, that we may regard the latter, his kinsman as descended from Swerting, as his immediate successor. Indeed I have little doubt, that Ælle is the person, who is named in the mysterious lines, which occur, entirely without context, near the beginning of the poem:—

"I heard that the queen of Ela, the consort of the warlike
"Scylfing:"[34]—

For we learn from the speech of Beowulf's thane, cited above, that the Scylfings renewed their feud with the Geats immediately after Beowulf's death, and this Ela was a Scylfing. That he was so, does not in the least impugn his identity with Ælle of Deira, the descendant of Swerting. For the Geats and Scylfings were connected by the ties of kindred; Weohstan is said to have slain his kinsman, the son of Ohthere; Wiglaf, his son, is called a prince of the Scylfings; and they were of the same family as Beowulf, the Wægmundings. What the precise relationship between these races was, can only be matter of conjecture; but as the alternative is presented to us, that Hrethel was the brother, or that he married the sister of Swerting, we may adopt the latter in preference; and thus Hrethel and Hygelac would be con-

---

[34] F. 130.

nected by marriage with the ancestry of Ælle, and Ecgtheow and Beowulf, Weohstan and Wiglaf, probably descended directly from the same stock.

Hrethel and his family appear to have been in Yorkshire first, where also we have found the Scylfings; a feud was commenced between them which may have compelled the former to seek a new home; after Hrethel's death his sons undertook an expedition against the Scylfings; the Scylfings in their turn invaded the territory of the Geats, after the death of Hygelac; Beowulf repulsed them, carried the war into their country, and subdued them; and lastly, as it appears, they renewed the conflict, after his death, and were victorious. For so the conclusion of the speech, of which part has been already quoted, informs us:—

"Now the war-leader has laid down laughter, sport and "joy of song. Therefore the spear will be brandished with "hands, raised in hands, many a morning cruel. The warrior "shall not waken the sound of the harp; but the wan raven, "busy over the dead, shall chatter much, shall tell the eagle, "how it sped with him at his feast, when with the wolf he "plundered the slain."[35]

And the poet confirms it with a comment of his own:—

"So the bold warrior was saying, of evil forebodings; he "belied not much of fates or words."

Now as Ela was a Scylfing; as the Scylfings were victorious over the Geats after Beowulf's death, which occurred about the time of Ælle's accession; as Hrethel's family were connected with the ancestors of Ælle; and as Beowulf's ancestors were Scylfings, it seems fair to conclude, that Ela of the

---

[35] F. 195.

poem is Ælle of the history of Deira. Where then shall we find Scylf the ancestor of his race? It is not improbable that the Cambrian genealogist has given his name more correctly than the Anglo-Saxon chronicler; that he is the person whom the former calls Zegulf, the latter Sæfugel, and of whom as the cotemporary and associate of Hencgest, we have found traces in Yorkshire and elsewhere. Thus does the history of Beowulf bring us to the commencement of the authentic history of Northumbria; the chain of probabilities which enable us to claim him for England is complete; and may fairly be considered as amounting to something like certainty, when all the circumstances are taken into account.

Two or three names still remain to be noticed. In Beowulf's last conflict he was assisted by a young warrior, one of his comrades:—

"Wiglaf was he called, son of Weoxstan,[36] a lovely shield-
"warrior, prince of the Scylfings, kinsman of Ælfhere. He
"saw his liege-lord suffer heat under his war-helm. He re-
"membered then the benefit that he had granted him before,
"the wealthy dwelling-place of the Wægmundings, every
"folk-right, as his father had possessed it. He might not
"then refrain, he took his yellow linden shield, drew his old
"sword———. He[37] held the ornaments many half-years,
"the bill and the byrnie; until his son might achieve earl-
"ship as his father before him. He gave him then among
"the Geats numberless war-weeds of every kind, when he,
"sage, betook him on his way forth from life."[38]

---

[36] Weohstan or Wihstan (readings which occur in other passages) are doubtless better than Weoxstan. The x in the latter can only represent the Runic *Gifu* or *Gear*.

[37] Weohstan.   [38] F. 188.

Farther on, Beowulf says to him:—

" Thou art the last of our race, of the Wægmundings." [39]

We have four traces of a person named Wihstan, nearly in a line; Wistaston in Herefordshire, Wistanstow and Westanswick in Shropshire, and Wistaston in Cheshire; and it is very probable that he was the Wihstan of our poem; for, in close proximity to Wistanstow, we have traces of the Geats and Hrethlings, in the names of the township of Gatton, and of the parish of Ratlinghope, of which it forms a part. This district, then, may have been one of the scenes of his military career. Wiglaf inherited the spoils of Eanmund from his father, and Beowulf granted to him the home of the Wægmundings, Wymondham in Norfolk. He accompanied Beowulf to the North.

Wulf and Eofer, the sons of Wonred, were chiefs high in the favour of Hygelac, and doubtless would accompany Beowulf when he went to reign over the Scyldings. It was about the beginning of the sixth century that they signalized themselves in the war with the Scylfings; and, towards the middle of it, a chieftain of the name of Wulf appears to have been engaged in wars with the Cambrian Britons. He is noticed in one of the poems in praise of Urien of Rheged; and as the son of Wonred is the only person of the name with whom we are acquainted, as his presence in the North is easily accounted for by his connection with Beowulf, and as he may reasonably be supposed to have been living at the time, we may with great probability suppose him to be the same person. The poem appears to contain an enumeration

---

[39] F. 191.

of Urien's successes over the Angles, before which these lines occur, naming Wulf as his antagonist:—

" O ddreig ddylaw adnaw doethaw " Don	" Of the chiefs owned by us, the " wisest was Don,
" yn i ddoeth Wlph yn dreis ar ei " alon	" When Wlph came to spoil his foes,
" hynny ddoeth Urien yn edydd " yn Aeron."	" When Urien came in the day in " Aeron."

After the mention of eight battles, these lines follow:—

" Atveilaw gwyn goruchyr cyd " mynan	" Decayed is the fair sovereignty " of the united (tribes),
" Eingl eddyl gwyrthryd	" The purpose of the Angles is hos- " tile,
" Lledrudd a gyfranc ag Wlph " yn rhyd."	" Slaughtering and contest and " Wlph in the road." [40]

We have now concluded our notice of the heroes of this poem, and the following table exhibits their relationship, and their connection with their cotemporaries, the fathers of the Anglo-Saxon royal dynasties. Healfdene's family settled in Northumbria in the fourth century; he was cotemporary with Hencgest I. and connected with Hencgest II; his dy-

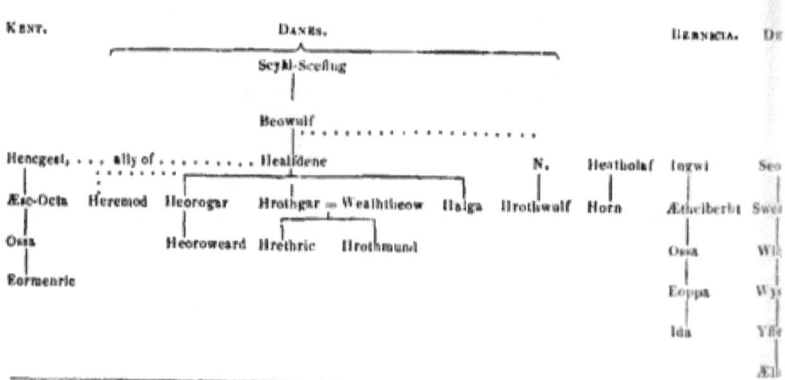

[40] I give these lines as translated by Mr. Nash in his excellent work " Taliesin." Mr. Stephens of Merthyr Tydvil has furnished me with a

nasty, in the persons of his grandsons, perished about the time of Eoppa's invasion, and probably in conflict with him. Seomel established himself in Deira, and founded Samlesbury in the fifth century; his son Swearting was the brother-in-law of Hrethel, and Swearting's fourth descendant, Ælle, was the successor of Hrethel's grandson, Beowulf, in Deira. Hrethel, Hygelac, and Beowulf reigned in Suffolk; feuds with the family of Wiwa, the founder of the East-Anglian kingdom, and the fall of Hrothgar's race, occasioned Beowulf's return to Deira. Hygelac appears to have married the widow of Offa; Heatholaf and Horn were cotemporary with Hrothgar.

Such are the indications, which the poem presents, of the connection of its heroes with the ancestors of five of the Anglo-Saxon royal dynasties, and the reader will see that they are quite consistent with the genealogies. The author also mentions Eormenric, the ancestor of the kings of Kent, of whom we shall have more to say in the following chapter.

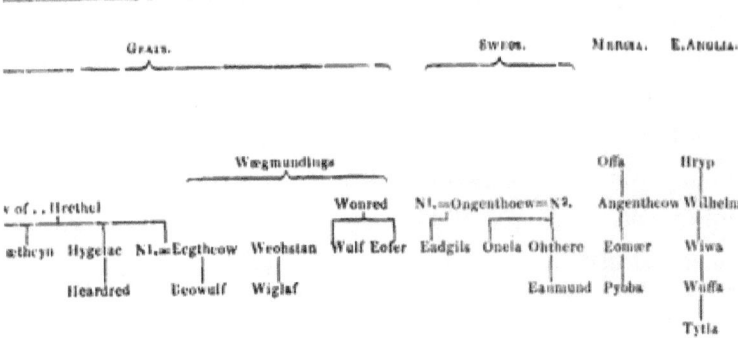

translation of the last, " the red-stained hero will slay Wlph at the ford," which has at least the advantage of being more intelligible.

As we have connected the reign of Beowulf with the times of Ida and of Ælle, the chronological succession of the kings of Bernicia and Deira may fitly conclude this chapter.

The names of the sons of Ida are variously stated. The Cambrian genealogist says they were twelve, whose names are " Adda, Eadlric, Deodric, Edric, Deothere, Osmer, of one " queen Bearnoch, Ealric." This list, therefore, is incomplete. Florence of Worcester also, in his Chronicle, and in the Appendix, mentions twelve; Adda, Baelric, Theodric, Æthelric, Osmær, and Theodhere, sons of his queen; Occa, Alric, Ecca, Oswald, Sogor, and Sogothere, sons of concubines. Thus he supplies what is wanting in the Cambrian's list, and vindicates the correction, " ex unâ reginâ" for " et " unam reginam," proposed by Mr. Stevenson.

The oldest authorities,—the Cambrian genealogist, and the compiler of the Chronological Notes, which are appended to More's MS. of Bæda,—are nearly agreed as to this succession:—

Glappa one year, Adda eight, Æthelric four, Theodric seven, Frithuwald six, Hussa seven; (the reign of Glappa being given by the latter authority only).

But the Cambrian adds a note, which distinctly marks the period of Frithuwald's reign,—" in whose time the kingdom " of the Kentishmen received baptism, by the mission of Gre- " gory;" and this shows that there is some mistake. On the other hand, Florence of Worcester's statement gives us a perfectly consistent chronology, enables us to verify the Cambrian's note with regard to Frithuwald, and to account for the government of Deira after the death of Ælle. I accept it, therefore, in preference; and as the united reigns of Æthelric, Frithuwald, and Hussa, as stated by the Cambrian, exactly supply the interval between the death of Ælle, A.D. 588, and Æthelfrith's usurpation of Deira, A.D. 605, I take these three names as those of Ælle's successors in Deira, and Florence's succession as that of Bernicia.

BERNICIA.		DEIRA.	
A.D.	Years.		Years.
547 Ida	12		
558		Ælle	30
559 Adda	7		
566 Clappa	5		
571 Theodwulf	1		
572 Frithuwulf	7		
579 Theodric	7		
586 Æthelric, son of Ida	7		
588		Æthelric, son of Adda	4
592		Frithuwald	6
593 Æthelfrith	24		
597	Arrival of S. Augustine.		
598		Hussa	7
605	conquers Deira.	Æthelfrith	12
617 Eadwine, succeeds to both kingdoms.			

By this scheme the different statements are nearly reconciled, and the succession of the kings of Deira, over which Æthelfrith did not gain the supremacy, until he had reigned twelve years in Bernicia, is satisfactorily accounted for. Florence seems to have confounded two Æthelrics, the son of Ida, and the son of Adda, when he says, that the former, after the death of Ælle, expelled Eadwine, and reigned in Deira; for Æthelfrith, the son of Æthelric, was not king of Deira until seventeen years afterwards; and the expulsion of Eadwine, and the seizure of his inheritance, are elsewhere ascribed to him, with greater probability. For Eadwine, born in A.D. 586, was incapable of reigning at his father's death; but was old enough to assert his claim in A.D. 605, which was certainly the date of the commencement of Æthelfrith's twelve years' reign in Deira. I believe it was also the date of the termination of Hussa's reign, which could not have been prolonged beyond this date, nor have ended more than a year earlier; since A.D. 597, the date of S. Augustine's coming, must fall within the reign of Frithuwald, his predecessor. The little that is known of the history of these princes will find its place in the concluding chapter of this work.

APPENDIX.

R. SHARON TURNER, no doubt, expresses the general feeling with regard to these dragon-stories, when he says, that "giants and dragons have no place in au-
"thentic history;" yet there are not wanting authors, and they in no-wise liable to the imputation of over-credulity, who do not hesitate to avow their conviction that they may have been founded in facts, and be substantially true.

Thus Mr. Howitt hints, that "individuals of the fast-de-
"caying genera, now known only in a fossil state, may have
"grown to an enormous size in the morasses of the North,
"and truly been a terror to the country."

Mrs. Jameson remarks, that "the dragon may have been,
"as regards form, originally a fact, because whether the scene
"of these dragon-legends be laid in Asia, Africa, or Europe,
"the imputed circumstances are little varied; and the dragon
"introduced in early painting and sculpture, is so invariably
"a gigantic winged crocodile, that it is presumed there must
"have been some common consent, and that the type may
"have been some fossil remains of the Saurian species, or
"even some far-off dim tradition of one of these tremendous
"reptiles."

Mr. Walbran, speaking of the Sockburn and Lambton worms, says, "It is not altogether unreasonable to suppose, "that in these, and other similar instances, some such crea- "tures did really exist, though their powers and appearance, "like many by-gone circumstances, of the authenticity of "which we are perfectly assured, were magnified and misre- "presented, in their transmission through centuries, by the "ignorance of the narrators."

Mr. Longstaffe, in a series of interesting papers on the tra- ditions of Durham, in which the opinions of these writers are cited as above, after saying that the Durham worms are only gigantic amphibious animals of the snake kind, suggests the following pertinent queries:— "Take them as symbols, "whence arose the symbol? The facts are laid at no very "distant period; had they referred to human dragons, would "not the facts have been recorded in history? Why are we "to discredit narratives of monstrous serpents, any more than "those of wolves and boars?"[1] In another place he says,— "The dates of these legends are so recent, that it seems next "to impossible, (if rovers or tyrants be typified), that the "symbolized events should not have been chronicled."

Again, in a memoir "On Durham before the Conquest," he observes, "Durham had no lack of monsters. Its worms, "enormous serpents of amphibious habits, gave employment "to the heroes of Lambton, Sockburn, and other places; if "we may believe that the legends, which with all the "attendant evidence, scarcely reach above the mediæval

---

[1] Mr. Longstaffe particularly refers to the fact of the capture of a monstrous boar, commemorated by the dedication of an altar to Silvanus, found at Stanhope in Weardale

"period, have a groundwork of truth. To explain them
"away, with the existence of enormous British serpents in
"the last geological strata, and corroborations of similar le-
"gends, as to other wild animals, before us, is no easy task."

A brief notice of some of these legends will be the best illustration of these remarks.

In the tenth century, (for that seems to have been his æra), Guy, Earl of Warwick, killed a winged dragon in Northumberland.

Before the Conquest, an ancestor of the Conyers family killed a dragon at Graystanes, in the parish of Sockburn. The manor of Sockburn was granted to this family by Ralph Flambard, Bishop of Durham, (A. D. 1099-1133), and has been held ever since by the service, of the lord of the manor meeting the bishop at Neasham ford, on his first entrance into his diocese, and presenting a sword, in memory of the event.

A.D. 1133, Gilles de Chin, lord of Berlaimont, slew a dragon which dwelt in a cave, near the village of Wasme, and in memory thereof, an annual procession was established at Mons.

In the thirteenth century, John, son of Roger de Somerville, of Wichnor in Staffordshire, killed a dragon, by means of a wheel, to which burning peats were attached, fixed on the point of a spear; with this he charged the monster, and left it fixed in his body, inflicting thus a mortal wound. For this he was knighted by William the Lion, made his chief falconer, and lord of the manor of Linton, in Roxburghshire, in which the encounter took place.

In the fourteenth century, when the Knights of S. John conquered Rhodes, a dragon is said to have dwelt in a den, on the brink of a morass, at the foot of Mount S. Stephen. Several knights, who had ventured to attack it, had fallen victims, and the Grand Master prohibited the rest from attempting so dangerous an enterprise. One alone, Deodato de Gozon, ventured to disobey, resolved to rid the island of the monster, or die. Having made himself, by reconnoitring it at a distance, familiar with its form, he had a model of it constructed, and trained two young bull-dogs to seize it by the belly, whilst he charged it with his lance. When they were perfect in this exercise, he rode down with them to the marsh, leaving some confidential attendants in a place, whence they could watch his proceedings in security. As the dragon ran to meet him, he charged it, but the monster's scales turned the point of his lance, and, his horse becoming unmanageable through terror, he was compelled to dismount, and continue the conflict with his sword. A stroke of the monster's tail felled him to the ground, and he was on the point of being devoured by it, when his bull-dogs seized it as they had been taught, and afforded him an opportunity of recovering his footing, and burying his sword in its body. Mortally wounded, the dragon reared in its agony, fell upon him, and would have crushed him to death, had not his attendants come to his assistance, and rescued him. On his return to the city, the people received him with triumph, but the Grand Master had him committed to prison, and brought to trial for disobedience; and it was only at the urgent entreaties of his council, that he consented to commute the sentence of death, for one of deprivation of the habit, and expulsion from the order. Deodato was accordingly deprived, but was afterwards restored, and eventually, in A. D. 1346, became one of the most illustrious Grand

Masters of the Order. He died A.D. 1353, and on his tomb, which remained in the Church of S. John at Rhodes, until the city fell into the hands of the Turks, his conflict with the dragon was represented, with the inscription DRAGONIS EXTINCTOR. This story at least appears to be sufficiently matter of fact, and free from exaggeration.

Thomas Walsingham relates, that, in A.D. 1344, a Saracen physician offered his services to Earl Warren, for the destruction of a serpent, which was committing depredations at Bromfield in the Welsh Marches, and destroyed it by his medical skill.

In the fifteenth century, another knight of Rhodes, Sir John Lambton, is said to have slain a dragon at Lambton in Durham; and, because he neglected the fulfilment of his vow, to kill the first living creature that should meet him afterwards, (for it was his father that met him), to have entailed a curse on nine generations of his family, which seems to have taken effect.

With these, and other stories of the same kind before us, forming, as it were, a consecutive chain of evidence of the existence of these creatures, it is impossible not to feel the force of Mr. Longstaffe's remark, that it is no easy task to explain them away. There seems no reason, why a race of dragons may not have once existed, like the Irish Elk and other wild animals, in this country, the Dodo in the Mauritius, and the Dinornis in New Zealand; and it is worthy of remark, how many of these stories are connected with the northern counties, as if the race had longest survived in those districts. The habitation of the Sockburn worm appears to have been in the immediate neighbourhood of the scene of Beowulf's adventure, the account of which at one time I felt inclined to explain, by the supposition that Beowulf fell a victim to mephitic vapours, collected in the recesses of a chambered tumulus, which he plundered; but which, after the perusal of the evidence collected by Mr. Longstaffe, and with the conviction on my mind, that the author of the poem lived very near to the times of his hero, I am compelled to admit may have had its foundation in fact, whatever amount of exaggeration it may contain.

CHAPTER VIII.

The Lament of Deor ; the Tale of the Traveller.

HE Lament of Deor, in the Exeter Book, is a relic of Anglo-Saxon poetry, inferior in value to no other. Adversity, which had befallen him, gave him occasion to seek comfort in the reflection, that as Weland and Beadohild, Geat and Mæthhild, Theodric and Eormanric's people, had surmounted their woes, so he might his own; and prompted him to write this poem, supplying an important link in the chain of evidence, which connects these personages with the history of our country.

I have already expressed my conviction, that Weland, as well as his father and brother, accompanied Horsa and Hencgest throughout their career of conquest. The traditions of England, Scandinavia, France, and Germany, celebrate his skill as a goldsmith and armourer; as such he would be an invaluable auxiliary to the forces of the invaders of Britain; and if, in romances, heroes of a later period are said to have possessed weapons of his forging, in our poems, which contain the earliest notices of him, kings and chieftains who flourished in the fifth and sixth centuries, are said to have owned these treasures. It is impossible to trace the traditions which relate to him beyond the fifth century.

In Beowulf, the hero's coat of mail, the legacy of Hrethel, is said to have been his work; in the story of Horn, the hero receives from Riminild a sword of his forging; in the recently discovered fragments of the saga of Waldhere, we have allusions to his sword Minming, his father-in-law Nithhad, and his son Widia; and in that curious collection of early traditions, the Life of Merlin, Rhydderch, king of Cumbria, is represented as commanding cups to be produced, which Weland chased in the city Sigeni.[1] The last is most important, as evidence of a British tradition, that Weland resided in this country; for Sigeni was certainly in Britain, and its destruction is the subject of one of the predictions, ascribed in the same work to Merlin.[2]

It is probable that Weland received his name on account of his skill, for the Icelandic Voelundr, and the Ceylonese Velende, equally signify "smith;" and the verb *welan*, to " burn," to " be hot," &c. suggests its etymology.[3]

The Lament of Deor begins with an allusion to his misfortunes:—

" Weland knew in himself the worm of exile. The prudent
" chief endured sorrows; had grief and weariness, winter-
" cold wretchedness, for companions; oft experienced misery;
" after Nithhad had laid him, unhappy man, in captivity with
" a tough sinew-band."

" Her brothers' death was not so sore in mind to Beado-

---

[1] " Pocula quæ sculpsit Guielandus in urbe Sigeni." L. 235.

[2] " Urbs Sigeni et turres et magna palatia plangent
" Diruta." L. 614.

[3] It was certainly a personal name; borne amongst others by a chieftain who had been in England, and invaded France in A.D. 861.

" hild, as her own affair, that she had discovered certainly
" that she was pregnant. Never might she think assuredly,
" how that could happen."

Mr. Thorpe has justly remarked, that the greater simplicity of the story, as alluded to in these passages, over that in the Edda, speaks strongly in favour of its greater antiquity; and the fact, that we have it in its simplest and most ancient form in our language, gives us an additional claim to Weland. Still from the Edda we may gather a few particulars, sufficient to explain these allusions, viz. that Nithhad, coveting the wealth of Weland, beset his dwelling, took him prisoner, and conveyed him to an island, where he compelled him to work for him; that Weland took revenge by murdering the sons of Nithhad, and violating his daughter Beadohild, whilst under the influence of a narcotic potion, and then made his escape. Whether he afterwards took further revenge or not, does not appear; but Beadohild was recognized as his wife, and their son Wittich, Wudga, or Widia, plays a conspicuous part in other sagas.

Possibly the ancient fortress, Uffington Castle, in Berkshire, may have been the " urbs Sigeni" of the Life of Merlin, the residence of Weland; for a cromlech, a little more than a mile distant, bearing the name of Wayland's smithy, seems to indicate a traditional belief, that he dwelt in its neighbourhood; and this tradition is as old as the tenth century, for " Welandes smiththe," is mentioned in a charter of Eadræd, A. D. 955.[4] Wadley, a few miles to the north, bears the name of his father, and the Nythe farms, six miles to the west, may have been named after his enemy Nithhad.

Deor's next stanza introduces us to Geat and Mæthhild,

---

[4] Cod. Diplom. 1172.

who are wholly unknown to Scandinavian or German romance, but whose story was doubtless once familiar to our forefathers:—

"We have many times heard, that Geat's wooings to Mæthhild were endless, so that the pining love took away from him all sleep."

The scene of this story may have been in Oxfordshire, for a register of the boundaries of Wychwood forest gives us in close proximity, Gatesden, Madlebroc, and Madlewell. Traces of a Geat we have noticed elsewhere. Possibly he was the son of Vortigern, and grandson of Henegest, whom the triads call Gotta; but of Mæthhild I can find no other trace.

Then follow these notices of Theodric and Eormanric:—

"Theodric had not[5] Mæringaburg for thirty winters. That was known to many."

"We have heard of Eormanric's wolf-like mind. He possessed wide nations of the kingdom of the Goths. Many a warrior sat, bound with sorrows, anticipating calamity, wished enough that there were an end of that kingdom."

The identification of Theodric and Eormanric must be reserved for the present. We shall find them reigning in the districts in which Weland and Geat dwelt, but somewhat later.

Of himself Deor says:—

"A sorrowing one sits deprived of happiness; in his mind it grows dark; he thinks to himself that his share of woes is endless. Then may he think that the wise Lord changes enough, throughout the world. To many a chief he dispenses honour, constant success; to others a share of woes.

---

[5] I adopt, without hesitation, Mr. Coneybeare's suggestion that *ne* should be supplied,—
"Theodric ne áhte Mæringaburg."
Without it the stanza is unintelligible.

" That I will say of myself, that I was for a while the scóp
" of the Heodenings, dear to my lord. Deor was my name.
" I had a good following, a faithful lord, for many winters;
" until that now Heorrenda, a song-crafty man, has obtained
" the land-right, which the refuge of warriors gave to me
" before."

Heoden, whose name is retained by Hednesford in Staffordshire, and once was by Hedenesdene[6] in Hampshire, and who perhaps was one of the associates of Hencgest, was the father or lord of the Heodenings. Deor's own name occurs in the same district as those of all the persons he commemorates, at Deoran treów[7] in Berkshire; and perhaps Dirham in Gloucestershire may have been the land-right, the loss of which he laments. He does not go far from home, then, for illustrations of his theme, nor to very remote times; Weland, Nithhad, Geat, Mæthhild, Theodric, and Eormanric, may all be traced in the district in which Oxfordshire, Berkshire, Wiltshire, and Gloucestershire meet; and all lived in the fifth or sixth centuries.

As Deor then undoubtedly belongs to us, so also does Heorrenda, a scóp whose accomplishments are celebrated in several Teutonic sagas.

The Traveller's Tale, like many other pieces in the Exeter Book, is but a fragment of a larger poem. The first twenty lines introduce the Traveller to us, speaking of him in the third person, and giving parenthetically a brief notice of his origin, and of his journey, and perhaps an allusion to his subsequent fate.

" The Traveller spake, unlocked his word-hoard, he who

---

[6] C. D. 1063.   [7] Chron. Abingdon, i. 146.

"had met most tribes over the earth, travelled through na-
"tions. Oft he had received in hall a memorable gift. No-
"bles gave birth to him, from among the Myrgings. He
"with Ealhhild, the faithful peace-weaver, in his first journey
"sought the abode of the Hreth-king, Eormanric, the hostile
"faith breaker, east of Ongle. He began then much to
"speak."[8]

Then follows, in the first person, the Traveller's own account of his wanderings. I shall endeavour first to determine the period of his journey, to identify as far as possible the peoples whom he mentions, and to ascertain the country to which he belonged; and shall then be able to show the bearing of this poem on the history of our country.

The time, then, is distinctly limited by his mention of Theodric,[9] the son of Chlodovech, who reigned over the Franks from A. D. 511 to 534. His journey, therefore, was made after Theodric's accession to the throne, and all the circumstances of his story lead to the conclusion, that it was during the earlier part of Theodric's reign.

He commences his story with a list of illustrious princes, some of whom he afterwards tells us that he visited. With one exception, all these are of Barbaric race, and, as far as they can be identified, lived either before or during the time which is indicated by this notice of Theodric. The exception is:—

"Alexandreas richest of all of the race of men."[10]

And the Traveller says:—

"He most prospered of those whom I have heard of over
"the earth."

---

[8] L. 1-20.   [9] L. 49.   [10] L. 31-36.

It is not, of course, Alexander of Macedon who is here meant; it is not likely that he would be mentioned in the company of princes, all of whom flourished in the fifth and sixth centuries; he is very probably that Alexander of whom Procopius speaks, who, having raised himself from an humble station, took a prominent part in the affairs of the empire at this period, was employed confidentially by the Emperors, and was notorious for his wealth and avarice.

Of the rest,—Fin Folcwalding[11] was killed about the middle of the fifth century, and Ongentheow,[12] king of the Sweos, about its close, or the beginning of the sixth; Wada[13] of the Hælsings, and Sceafa[14] of the Longbeards, were probably companions of the first Hencgest; Alewih[15] of the Danes, and Witta of the Swæfs,[16] were the antagonists of Offa; Offa,[17] Breoca,[18] Hrothgar and Hrothwulf[19] were all living about the beginning of the sixth century; and Ætla,[20] Eormanric,[21] Gifica,[22] and Hagena,[23] were, as will be shown in the sequel, the Traveller's cotemporaries.

That he travelled on the continent, is admitted of course; but it is equally certain that this island was the scene of some part at least of his wanderings, for he tells us that he was with the Scots and Picts. If then we had no evidence to the fact, that others of the races whom he mentions were actually settled in this country, we might have presumed that some of them were so, for a Teutonic noble would hardly have mentioned a Celtic people whom he found here, and have omitted all notice of the tribes of his own race. Now a very large proportion of those whom he visited, must have

---

[11] L. 55.   [12] L. 64.   [13] L. 46.   [14] L. 66.   [15] L. 72.
[16] L. 45.   [17] L. 71.   [18] L. 51.   [19] L. 91.   [20] L. 37.
[21] L. 40.   [22] L. 42.   [23] L. 159.

been, at one time or another, amongst the colonists of Britain; and they were most probably here at the time of his journey, for the evidence of Procopius shows, that the colonization of Britain was so complete, only a few years later, that the Anglo-Saxon race were already forced to seek fresh settlements in Gaul. He says:—

" Three very numerous nations, the Angili, Frissones, and "those named from the island Brittones, over each of which "a king presides, possess Brittia. So great, indeed, appears "to be the fecundity of these nations, that every year vast "numbers, migrating thence with their wives and children, "go to the Franks, who locate them in such places as seem "the most desolate of their country."[24]

The story of Hadugot also, which will be noticed in the sequel, is evidence of the same fact, that the tide of emigration, which had flowed steadily from the continent to Britain during the fifth century, was returning in the sixth; and we have many indications, in the occurrence of the names of the same families, in the eastern and southern counties of England, and on the opposite coasts of the Continent, of this emigration of the Angles to Gaul.[25]

Now of the tribes or families, whom the Traveller visited or mentions, we find traces in this country of the following; and if the names of some of them be found on the Continent also, it is most likely that they were in England at the time

---

[24] De Bello Gothico, IV.
[25] As, for example, these—

Bainghem	Bingham.	Haffreingue	Havering.	Lozinghem	Loseley.
Balinghem	Ballingdon.	Halinghen	Halling.	Marcoing	Markington.
Bellaing	Bellingham.	Hardinghem	Hardingham.	Mazenghem	Massingham.
Bazinghem	Basingstoke.	Harlingen	Harling.	Molinghem	Mollington.
Bezinghem	Bessingham.	Hocquinghem	Hucking.	Nabringhem	Nafferton.
Boesinghe	Bossington.	Hondeghem	Huntingdon.	Racquinghem	Rackham.
Dringham	Dringoe.	Inghem	Ingham.	Rudinghem	Reading.
Echinghem	Eckington.	Ledringhem	Letheringham.	Teteghen	Teddington.
Eringhem	Erringden.	Leffrinchouke	Leverington.	Totinghem	Tooting.

of his journey, whether those names indicate their original homes whence they came hither, or the settlements which they formed in the reign of Theodric.

AMOTHINGAS. Emmotland in Yorkshire, anciently " æt Eamotum;"[26] perhaps also Amotherley, also in Yorkshire.

BANINGAS. Bæningesburg,[27] now Banbury Camp, and Benningwyrth,[28] now Bengeworth, Worcestershire; Banningham, Norfolk; Benningborough and Benningholme, Yorkshire; Bennington, Hertfordshire; and Bennington, Lincolnshire.

BRONDINGAS. In Suffolk, subjects of Brecca, already noticed.

CREACAS. Cracoe, Craike, and Crakehall, Yorkshire; Creake, Norfolk; Crakemarsh, Staffordshire.

DENAS, or DENINGAS. Denford, Northamptonshire; Dentons in Northamptonshire, Huntingdonshire, Lincolnshire, Yorkshire, Lancashire, Northumberland, Kent, Sussex, and Derbyshire; Denhams in Suffolk and Buckinghamshire; Denbury in Devonshire. The lord of the Denas, mentioned in this poem, was Alewih, the enemy of Offa; Hrothgar's subjects are called Denas or Deningas, and Gaimar speaks of Danes as settled in Norfolk.

ENGLAS. Anglesey, Cambridgeshire; Anglesey island; Englefield, Berkshire; Englewood Forest. The Englas, in this poem, were subjects of Offa.

EOLAS. Youlthorpe and Youlton, Yorkshire; Youlgrave,

---

[26] Sax. Chron. A. D. 926. [27] Cod. Diplom. 148.
[28] Ibid. 61, &c.

Derbyshire. There was also a village in Huntingdonshire, called "æt Eolum."[29]

EOWAS. Ewshott, Hampshire.

FINNAS. Findern, Derbyshire; Finney, Yorkshire; Finborough, Suffolk.

FRESAS. Already noticed, as associated with the Angles in the invasion of Britain.

GEATAS. Gatton, Shropshire; Gatton, Surrey; Gatcombe, Wight.

GEFFLEGAS. Gifle,[30] Devonshire; Yeaveley, Derbyshire. The latter is probably the "Gyfla" or "Eyfla" of 300 hides, mentioned in the "Numerus Hidarum."

GEFTHAS. Iffley,[31] Oxfordshire; Gipton, Yorkshire. They are mentioned in Beowulf, in terms which indicate that they were settled in this country.

HÆLSINGAS. Helsington, Westmoreland; Elsing,[32] Norfolk.

HEATHO-BEARDAS and LONG-BEARDAS. Heatho being merely a prefix indicative of their warlike character, Ettmüller supposes the Heatho-Beardas to have been of the same race as the Long-Beardas. The former are only mentioned by the Traveller when he alludes to their defeat at Heort; the latter he visited. This nation appears to have given name to the Bardfields, Essex; Bardwell, Suffolk; Bardsea, Lancashire; and Bardsea[33] island, Caernarvonshire.

---

[29] Cod. Diplom. 599.
[30] Ibid. 314, 1290.
[31] Givetelei, Domesday.
[32] Helsinga, Domesday.

[33] It is evident that the three islands, Anglesey, Bardsey, and Ramsey, derive their names from the Englas, Heatho-Beardas, and Heatho-Ræmis; and that the commonly received derivation of the second must be set aside.

HEATHO-RÆMIS. Ramsey, Huntingdonshire; Ramsden, Yorkshire; Ramshope, Northumberland; Ramsholt, Suffolk; Ramsden and Ramsey, Essex; Ramsgate, Kent; Ramsbury, Wiltshire; Ramsey island, Pembrokeshire.

HEREFARAS. Harberton, Devonshire.

HERELAS or HERELINGAS. Harlthorpe, and Harlington, Yorkshire; Harle, Northumberland; Harling, Norfolk; Arlington, Sussex; Harlton, Cambridgeshire; Harlington, Bedfordshire; Harlington, Middlesex; Arlington and Harlingham, Gloucestershire; and Arlington, Devonshire.

HOCINGAS. Hucking, Kent.

HREADAS or HREADINGAS. Readabeorh;[34] Radfield, Cambridgeshire; Radford, Nottinghamshire; Radford, Oxfordshire; Radford and Radway, Warwickshire; Radley, Berkshire; Radwell, Bedfordshire; Radwell, Hertfordshire; Reading, Berkshire; Raddingham, Somersetshire.

HRONAS or HRONINGAS. Runhall, Runham, Runton, Norfolk; Runwell, Essex; Runnington, Somersetshire; Runningmead, Surrey.

HUNAS. Hunton, Yorkshire; Huncoat, Lancashire; Hunwick, Durham; Hunworth, Norfolk; Hundon, Suffolk; Hunton, Kent; Huncote, Leicestershire.

HUNDINGAS. Huntingdon; Huntingdon, Yorkshire; Huntington, Cheshire; Huntingdun,[35] Leicestershire; Huntington, Staffordshire; Huntington, Herefordshire; Huntingfield, Suffolk.

---

[34] Cod. Diplom. 100.   [35] Ibid. 473, 1330.

IDUMINGAS. The name of a person, who might be the ancestor of this family, occurs at Idmiston,[36] Wiltshire, and this perhaps was their settlement.

LEONAS. Leonberg;[37] Lenborough and Linford,[38] Buckinghamshire; Lenham, Kent; Lenton, Nottinghamshire; Lintons, Linthorpe, and Linthwaite, Yorkshire; Linacre, Lancashire; Linley, Derbyshire; Linton, Cambridgeshire.

RUMWALAS. Rumbruge,[39] Hampshire; Rumworth, Lancashire; Rumburgh, Suffolk; Romford, Essex. The name of the first may indicate a residence of this family in Hampshire, in which county also is the next place the Traveller mentions, Eatule, now Yateley. The Rumwalas have been supposed to be the Romans of Italy, on account of this Eatule, (which has also been understood to be Italy), occurring in context with this name; but, besides that it is inconceivable that the word Italia could be represented under this form, the Traveller would hardly have said, "also I was in Italy," after he had said, "I was with the Romans." The Rumwalas may indeed have been the Roman race in Britain, who of course were not extinct, at the time of the Traveller's journey.

RONDINGAS. Perhaps Roudingas, Tacitus' Reudingi, a tribe coterminous with the Angli in his days; Rodings, Essex; Rodington, Shropshire.

RUGAS. Rugawic;[40] Rugby, Warwickshire.

SEAXAS. Saxby, Lincolnshire; Saxton, Yorkshire; Sax-

---

[36] Idemestun, Domesday.
[38] Leonaford, Asser.
[37] Cod. Diplom. 284.
[39] Cod. Diplom. 992.
[40] Ibid. 123.

thorpe, Norfolk; Saxham and Saxtead, Suffolk; Saxby, Leicestershire.

SYCGAS or SECGAS. Sedgefield, Durham; Sedgewick, Westmoreland; Sedgeford, Norfolk; Sedgeley, Staffordshire; Sedgemoor, Worcestershire.

SERCINGAS. Their name appears combined with that of the Angles in Anglezark, Lancashire, and alone in the island of Sark.

SERINGAS. Sharrington, Norfolk; Sherrington, Buckinghamshire.

SWÆFAS. Swaffhams and Swavesey, Cambridgeshire; Swaffham, Norfolk; Swefling, Suffolk; Swaton,[41] Lincolnshire; Suavetorp,[42] Yorkshire; Suevecamp,[43] Herefordshire.

SWEOS. Swayfield, Lincolnshire; Sway, Hampshire.

SWEORD-WERAS. These are the Suardones, neighbours of the Angli from the time of Tacitus. "Sweordora, 300 hides," occurs in the "Numerus Hidarum;" and we have Swarby, Lincolnshire; Swarland, Northumberland; Swardestone, Norfolk; Swerford, Oxfordshire; Sweord-hlincas,[44] Kent; Sweord-leáh,[45] Dorsetshire.

THROWENDAS. Troughend, Northumberland.

THYRINGAS. Thorington, Suffolk; Thorington, Essex.

WÆRNAS. Warnford, Northumberland; Warnham, Sussex; Warnborough and Warnford, Hampshire.

WALAS. Walburn and Walden, Yorkshire; Walton in Staffordshire; and many other Waltons and Waldens.

---

[41] Suavetone, Domesday.   [42] Domesday.   [43] Ibid.
[44] Cod. Diplom. 199.   [45] Ibid. 260.

WENLAS.   Wendlebury, Oxfordshire; Wendel-hill, Yorkshire.

WINEDAS.   Windham, Sussex; Wendling, Norfolk; Wendover, Buckinghamshire.

WROSNAS.   Rossendale, Lancashire.

WYCINGAS.   Wycinges-mearc,[46] Canterbury; Wyke and Wycliffe, Yorkshire.

WOINGAS.   Wuhinga land,[47] Hampshire; Wing, Buckinghamshire; Wing, Rutlandshire; Wingfield, Derbyshire; Wingfield, Wiltshire; Wingfield, Suffolk; Wingham, Kent.

WULFINGAS or WYLFINGAS.   Wolfinges laéw,[48] Wiltshire; Wylfingaford.[49] These were the family of Herebrand, Hildibrand, and Heathobrand.

YMBRAS.   Imber, Wiltshire.

YTAS.   Itton, Monmouthshire; Ytinga ford,[50] and Yting stoc.[51]

Thus we find probable traces in this country of more than half the tribes or families whom the Traveller visited; and occasionally we find, in the neighbourhood of places which bear their names, other traces of the chieftains whom he mentions as their rulers, some of whom were his cotemporaries.

"Becca ruled the Banings,"[52]

and was visited by him.[53]   At the foot of Breedon hill, on which is the deserted earthwork, now called Banbury camp, anciently Bæninges-burg,[54] is Beckford. Bengeworth, an-

---

[46] Cod. Diplom. 3.   [47] Ibid. 624.   [48] Ibid. 460.
[49] Ibid. 1335.   [50] Ibid. 1257.   [51] Ibid. 1227.
[52] L. 39.   [53] L. 231.

[54] "Breodun, in cuius cacumine urbs est antiquo nomine Bæningesburg." Charter of Uhtred, king of the Hwiccas, A.D. 756. Cod. Diplom. 148.

ciently Benningewyrth, is about six miles distant from these; in the same county again we have Beccanleáh[55] near Honeybourn, and Beckbridge near Broadwas; and in the neighbouring county of Oxford, we have another Banbury and Beckley; so that it will readily be admitted that Becca's principality was in this district.

He mentions the Creacs and the Fins twice, and each time in context:—

"Casere ruled the Creacs, and Cælic the Fins;"[56]
and,

"I was with the Creacs, and with the Fins, and with
"Casere, who held sway of the joyous cities of Wiolan and
"the Wilns, and the kingdom of the Walas."[57]

These princes therefore were neighbours. Casere is certainly a Teutonic name, it was borne by the ancestor of the East-Anglian kings, and so probably by others besides this. I find, however, no trace of him, but of his subjects the Creacs, Wilns, and Walas, and of Wiolan I do; at Craykemarsh, Staffordshire, Great and Little Wilne in Derbyshire, Wilnecote in Warwickshire, Walton-on-Trent and another Walton, Willenhall, and perhaps Willington, in Staffordshire; and of his neighbours, Cælic and the Fins, at Calke and Findern in Derbyshire. A district comprising part of the three counties of Stafford, Warwick, and Derby, would seem to have been the territory of these chieftains.

Alewih, the lord of the Danes, has been already noticed.
"Hnæf ruled the Hocings."[58]

This is a different person from Healfdene's vassal, who fell at Finnesham, and who was not a Hocing, but the adversary of Fin, Hoce's son-in-law. About fourteen miles to the

---

[55] Cod. Diplom. 570.   [56] L. 41, 42.   [57] L. 153-158.   [58] L. 59.

north of Hocing-mæd[59] ("the field of Hoce") in Hampshire, was Hnæfleah[60] in Berkshire, and in the same district of Hampshire, Hnæfes scylf[61] near Crondall. The Hocings appear to have been amongst the families who emigrated to Gaul in the reign of Theodric, and Nebi and Huocingus are mentioned amongst the ancestors of one of the wives of Charlemagne.

"Helm ruled the Wulfings."[62]

The charter which supplies Wolfinges læw, gives us also Helmestreów in its neighbourhood.

"Wald ruled the Woings."[63]

Waltham in Hampshire, and Upwaltham in Sussex, are in the neighbourhood of "Wuhinga landæs hyrn;" in Kent we have a Waltham not far from Wingham; and in Essex, Wingford bridge connects the parishes of Great and Little Waltham.

"Holen ruled the Wrosns."[64]

Holen's name occurs at Hollin in Rossendale, and Hollinshead to the west of it, and at Hollins on the borders of Yorkshire, Lancashire, and Derbyshire.

"Hringweald was called king of the Herefaras."[65]

Four charters mention Hringwoldes beorg.[66] It was near Otterford, on the borders of Somersetshire and Devonshire, and in the latter county we have Harberton near Totness. Hringweald's name occurs also at Ringwold in Kent, perhaps at Ringwood in Hampshire, and at Hringwoldes treów[67] near Burcombe in Wiltshire, so that perhaps he was one of Hencgest's allies.

---

[59] Cod. Diplom. 1091. [60] Ibid. 430. [61] Ibid. 595.
[62] L. 60. [63] L. 61. [64] L. 68.
[65] L. 69, 70. [66] Cod. Diplom. 1051, 1052, 1117, 1140.
[67] Ibid. 1115.

"Mearchealf ruled the Hundings."[68]

There are two parishes named Marcle, a possible abbreviation of Mearchealf, about twelve miles from one of the Huntingtons, in Herefordshire.

"Thyle ruled the Rondings."[69]

There are three Tilburys, two to the south, and one to the north, of the district in Essex, in which we have noticed the Rodings.

"Billing ruled the Wærns."[70]

I have noticed this chieftain, as probably one of Hencgest's associates.

"Sceafthere ruled the Ymbras."[71]

The name of Shaftesbury, about eighteen miles from Imber, may be an abbreviation of Sceaftheresbyrig.

"Sceafa ruled the Longbeards."[72]

He also has been noticed, as probably a follower of Hencgest.

"Hagena ruled the Holm-kingdoms."[73]

This name occurs in Lincolnshire, at Hagnaby near Alford, and Hagnaby near Spilsby, both on the borders of the fen-country, which may well have been called Holm-rice; Hainton near Wragby, in the same county, may also have been named from him.

"Meaca ruled the Myrgings."[74]

We find the name of this prince at Mackley, close to Marchington, in Staffordshire, at Mackworth, near Markeaton, in Derbyshire, and again at Maxtoke in Warwickshire. The Myrgings are probably the same as the Myrcas,[75] who gave

---

[68] L. 48.   [69] L. 50.   [70] L. 52.   [71] L. 66.
[72] L. 67.   [73] L. 43.   [74] L. 47.

[75] So the Gothic royal race are called Amalas and Amalingas, and Hrothgar's subjects Denas and Deningas.

name to the kingdom of Mercia. Under the patronymic form of their name they have left few traces, but Mearcyncgseol, abbreviated to Markshall, suggests that a similar abbreviation may have taken place in other names. The Traveller distinguishes the Myrgings from the With-Myrgings. He was himself of a noble family among the former, and he says that he visited the latter,[76] and includes them among the subjects of Offa.[77] His feudal lord was Eadgils, whose name we find at Etchells in Cheshire; and if this prince were the same as Eadgils, who is mentioned in Beowulf, and who certainly was living at the same time, the presence of the Myrgings in Yorkshire would be accounted for.

In most of these instances, there can be little doubt, that the identity of the princes whom the Traveller mentions, is established, by the occurrence of their names in the same districts as those of the tribes, whom he represents as subject to them. His notices of them are, therefore, equally with those of Hrothgar and of Offa, already referred to, allusions to traditions current in England, for two only of them were visited by him; the rest probably lived before his time, and some of them as early as the days of Hencgest. Besides these, Whalley in Northumberland, Whalley in Lancashire, and Whaley in Cheshire, bear the name of

"Hwala once the best,"[78]

and Sigeres ác,[79] on the Ouse in Yorkshire, that of Sigehere, of whom he says:—

"Sigehere longest ruled the Sea-Danes."[80]

Many of the princes, too, whom he visited, may be shown

---

[76] L. 238.
[77] L. 86.
[78] L. 29, 30.
[79] Cod. Diplom. 480.
[80] L. 57, 58.

to have reigned in England. Thus Beadeca,[81] whose name we have found in Hampshire, Bedfordshire, and Derbyshire, the sixth descendant of Woden in the line of the East Saxons, might very well have survived until his days. As he was with the Englas,[82] Incgentheow,[83] whom he visited, was perhaps the son of Offa, whom the Cambrian genealogist calls Ongen, the Saxon Chronicle Angeltheow, and Florence, (apparently confounding him with a person who is named in the Bernician genealogy), Angengeat. Secca's[84] name occurs at Seccandún, now Seckington, in Warwickshire; Sifeca's[85] at Seofecandene,[86] near Burford, in Oxfordshire, (called Sewkedene in a document of A.D. 1300, which also mentions Sewkeford near it), at Seofecan wyrth,[87] now Seacourt, also in Oxfordshire, and at Seovechesham, now Abingdon, in Berkshire; Seafola's[88] probably at Sible Hedingham, and Sibleys, not far from it, in Essex; Hlithe's[89] at Lidbury camp on Salisbury plain, and at Liddington, in the same county, where there is a large fortress; Gislhere's[90] at Gislhereswyrth,[91] now Isleworth, in Middlesex; Hungar's[92] at Hungarton in Leicestershire, and Hungerford in Berkshire; Rædhere's[93] at Rattery in Devonshire; Elsa's[94] at Elsenham in Essex.

He gives us a particular notice of one of the princes who entertained him:—

"I was also in Eatule with Ælfwine, the son of Eadwine, "who had, in my opinion, of mankind the lightest hand to

---

[81] L. 235. [82] L. 123. [83] L. 234.
[84] L. 231. [85] L. 233. [86] Cod. Diplom. 570.
[87] Cod. Diplom. 1216. [88] L. 232. [89] L. 234.
[90] L. 248. [91] Cod. Diplom. 38. [92] L. 236.
[93] L. 247. [94] L. 235.

" win praise, the most generous heart in the distribution of
" rings, bright circlets."[95]

Eatule, I believe, is Yateley in Hampshire, in which district a prince named Ælfwine appears to have lived, whose territory extended about sixteen miles to the west, since Ælfwines mearc[96] was in the neighbourhood of Hannington. Idstone, near Ashbury in the adjoining county of Berkshire, was anciently Edwinestone.[97]

Thus it is certain that the Traveller was in England, and probable that a very large proportion, of those whose names he enumerates, were settled in the districts, which now form the counties of Cheshire, Derbyshire, Staffordshire, Warwickshire, Worcestershire, Gloucestershire, Oxfordshire, Wiltshire, Hampshire, and Berkshire. England, then, being ascertained to have been the scene of great part of his wanderings, and the period being indicated by his notice of Theodric, we are in a position to identify more of the personages whose names occur in his highly interesting narrative.

He says he was with Eadwine.[98] He, therefore, visited him in the course of his journey, and, as it would appear, conducted his daughter Ealhhild to the court of Eormanric, whose dominions were eastward of Ongle, the kingdom of Offa, (which, as we have seen, comprised Gloucestershire at this time). This Eadwine, whether the same person as the father of Ælfwine or not, (though it is more probable that he was not, since Ælfwine seems to have been an independent prince), may have been the chieftain, whose name is borne by

---

[95] L. 141-150.
[97] Domesday.
[96] Cod. Diplom. 939.
[98] L. 235.

two parishes, the Edwins in Herefordshire. If so, his territory would actually come within the compass of the Traveller's journey, since he was with the Hundings, traces of whom, with their prince Mearchealf, we have found in this county.

He thus describes his visit to Eormanric:—

"I was with Eormanric. There all the time the king
"of the Goths treated me well. He, the chieftain of his
"citizens, gave me a ring, whereon were marked six hundred
"sceats of beaten gold, in shilling-reckoning. That, when I
"came home, I gave to Eadgils, the prince of the Myrgings,
"my patron-lord, for a possession, for a recompense to my
"beloved, because he gave me land, my patrimony. And
"then Ealhhild, the noble lady-queen, the daughter of Ead-
"wine, gave me another (ring). I lengthened her praise
"through many lands, when I should say by song, where I
"knew under heaven the best gold-decked queen, dispensing
"gifts; when I and Skilling raised the song, with clear
"voice, for our victor-lord, our voice resounded loud to the
"harp. Then many men, proud in spirit, they who knew
"well, spake in words, that they had never heard better song.
"Thence I traversed all the country of the Goths. I always
"sought the best of journeys; that was the household band of
"Eormanric."[99]

This Eormanric, the cotemporary of Theodric the Frank, can be no other than the father of the first Christian king of Kent, Æthelberht. Æsc-Octa died in A.D. 491, and if twenty years are rightly assigned to the reign of Ossa, that of Eormanric would commence in A.D. 511, and he died pro-

---

[99] L. 177-224.

bably in A.D. 560. His dominions were eastward of Offa's. He is called king of the Goths, and rightly so; for the genealogies have shown us, that the royal dynasties of the Angles, Jutes, and Saxons, were of the same blood as those who ruled the Goths; and they enable us to understand how Oslac, the father-in-law of Ælfræd, was a Goth,[100] as descended from Stuf and Wihtgar, who were nephews of Cerdic king of the West Saxons, and whose followers, equally with the colonists of Kent, were Jutes; and what Belisarius meant, when he said, (as represented by Procopius), " we permit the Goths " to occupy Britain." [101] We even find in this country, in the name of Amalburn,[102] a trace of that which was the noblest race amongst the Goths, the family to which all the Ostrogothic kings belonged. This is, of course, the Eormanric, to whom one of Deor's stanzas refers.

In connection with the Hreadas, and their princes Wulfhere and Wyrmhere, the Traveller mentions an Ætla, apparently the same person as he who is said, in the beginning of the poem, to have ruled the Huns:—

" I sought Wulfhere and Wyrmhere full often. There war " ceased not, when the army of the Hrædas should defend with " hard swords, about the wood of the Wistlas, their old patri- " monial seat, from the folks of Ætla." [103]

Like other chieftains of the time, engaged in the innumerable wars of which Henry of Huntingdon speaks, Wulfhere and Wyrmhere appear to have moved from place to place. We find traces of their names, in connection with that of the

---

[100] " Oslac Gothus erat natione, ortus enim erat de Gothis et Jutis, de " semine scilicet Stuf et Wihtgar." ASSER.

[101] De Bello Gothico, II.   [102] Cod. Diplom. 685.
[103] L. 239-246.

Hrædas, repeatedly in different districts. In Warwickshire the names of Wulfhere and Ætla occur close together at Wolverheath, Wolvershill, and Attleborough, the former indicating perhaps no more than a temporary presence, the latter a fixed residence. In Cambridgeshire, Radfield hundred; in Suffolk, Westley, Westleton, and Woolverstone; and, north of these, in Norfolk, Wolverton and Wormegay; present traces of the Hreadas, Wistlas, Wulfhere and Wyrmhere. This may have been their proper country, and the scene of the war of which the Traveller speaks; for in Norfolk we have two places named after Ætla, Attlebridge and Attleborough, indicating perhaps that he settled there, after the expulsion of these people. In Buckinghamshire we have Wolverton, and Radcliffe; in Oxfordshire, Wolvercote, Radford, and Radcote; in Somersetshire, Wolverton, and Radstock; in Herefordshire, Wolverlow, Wormelow, Wormbridge, Wormsley, and Radlow.

This Ætla was the Traveller's cotemporary, and that he was, like his namesake, the historic Attila, a king of the Huns, is not impossible; for we have Hundon in Suffolk, and Hunworth in Norfolk, in the same district as Attlebridge, and Attleborough; and Huncote in Leicestershire, not far from the other Attleborough; and, four miles from this Huncote, we have a trace of another Hunnish name, Froila, at Frowlesworth. The sequel will confirm this.

The Traveller also speaks of having visited the Burgendas:—

"And I was with the Burgends; there I received a
"ring, there Guthhere gave me a welcome present, in reward
"of song; that was no sluggish king." [104]

---

[104] L. 131-136.

Now the kings of the Burgundians proper, at this time, were Sigismund, A.D. 516 to 524, and Godemar, A.D. 524 to 534, with whom their monarchy ceased.[105] They had no king whose name will answer to Guthhere, but Gundahari, who established their kingdom in Gaul, and was slain A.D. 436; and as Gundebald, promulgating his laws, in A.D. 502, makes mention of " our ancestors of royal memory, Gibica, Godo-" mar, Gislahari, and Gundahari : "—it is evident that the three former must have preceded Gundahari, his grandfather, in the ancient seats of their nation. The first, Gibica, has been identified with the individual of whom the Traveller speaks,[106] as having ruled the Burgends; but there was a Gifica once in England, who gave his name to Gifican cumb,[107] near Tisbury in Wiltshire. Indeed I am satisfied that a detachment of this nation effected settlements in this island;— perhaps immediately after that great revolution, which seated Gundebald on the throne, and in which Arthur appears to

---

[105] The succession of the Burgundian kings was as follows:—
A.D. 407, Gundahari passed the Rhine.
    413, was elected King by the whole nation. Slain by the Huns in
    436, Gundevech, his son, succeeding. He was followed by,
    473, Chilperic, his son, whose brothers Gundebald, Godemar, and Godegisl had principalities under him.
    490, Gundebald slew his three brothers, and the sons of Chilperic. In
    516, Sigismund, his son, succeeded him. In
    523, he was defeated by the Franks, and in
    524, was slain by them, with his sons Gislahari and Gundebald. Godemar, his brother, reigned after him ten years. In
    534, he was put to flight by the Franks, and it never was known what became of him. Did he find an asylum in England, and give name to Godmersham in Kent?

[106] L. 40.   [107] Cod. Diplom. 641.

have taken part. Of this band of refugees, or allies of Modred, Gifica may have been the leader; his relation to Guthhere and Gislhere will shortly appear.

The opportune discovery, and publication, by Mr. George Stephens of Copenhagen, of two leaves of an Anglo-Saxon saga, has supplied most important illustrations of this part of my subject. The first leaf contains the following passage:—

—" hýrde hyne georne.	—" heard him gladly.
" Húru Welandes worc	" At least Weland's work
" ne geswíceth monna ænigum,	" fails not any man,
" thára the Mimming can	" who can Mimming
" heárne gehealdan.	" shining hold.
" Oft æt hilde gedreás,	" Oft in battle fell,
" swát-fág and sweord-wúnd,	" blood-stained and sword- " wounded,
" sec æfter othrum.	" one warrior after another.
" Ætlan ord-wyga,	" Ætla's van-warrior!
" ne lǽt thín ellen nú gyt	" let not thy courage now yet
" gedreósan to dæge,	" fail to-day,
" dryhtscipe (feallan).	" thy lordship fall.
" Ac is se dag cumen,	" For the day is come,
" thæt thú scealt áninga other- " twéga	" that thou shalt wholly either
" líf for-leósan,	" lose thy life,
" oththe lange	" or long
" dóm ágan mid eldum,	" have power among men,
" Ælfheres sunu.	" Ælfhere's son!
" Nalles ic thé, wine mín,	" Never, I to thee, my friend,
" wordum cíthe thý,	" say it in words,
" ic thé gesáwe,	" saw I thee,
" æt thám sweord-plegan,	" at the sword-play,
" thurh edwitscype,	" through cowardice,
" æniges monnes	" of any man
" wig for-búgan,	" the combat decline,
" oththe on weal fléon	" or flee to fortress
" líce beorgan;	" thy body to defend;
" theah the láthra féla	" although many foes
" thínne byrn-homon	" thy mail-shirt
" billum heówun.	" hewed with bills.

" Ac thú symle furthor	" But thou ever further
" feohtan sóhtest,	" soughtest to fight,
" mæl ofer mearce;	" mark over border;[108]
" thá ic thé, metod, on-dréd,	" when I feared for thee, prince,
" thæt thú tó fýrenlice	" that thou too fiercely
" feohtan sóhtest,	" soughtest to fight,
" æt thám æt-stealle,	" at the battle-field,[109]
" othres monnes	" another man's
" wig-rædenne.	" war-counsellors.
" Weortha thé selfne	" Honour thyself
" gódum dædum,	" with good deeds,
" thenden thín gód recce.	" whilst thy good lasts.
" Ne murn thú for thí mece,	" Mourn not thou for the sword,
" the wearth máthma cyst,	" which was choicest of treasures,
" gifede to eóce unc.	" given us for aid.
" Thý thú Gúthhere	" For thou to Guthhere
" scealt beot for bígan,	" shalt his threat repel,
" thæs the he thás beaduwe	" for that he these quarrels
" ongan, mid unrýhte,	" began, with injustice,
" ærest sécan.	" first to seek.
" Forsóc he thám swurde,	" He forsook the sword,
" and thám sync-fatum,	" and the treasure-chests,
" beága mænigo;	" many rings;
" nú sceal, beága-leás,	" now shall, ring-less,
" hworfan from thisse hilde	" turn from this fight
" hláfurd, sécan	" the lord, to seek
" ealdne éthel,	" his old patrimony,
" oththe hér ǽr swefan.	" or here first sleep.
" Gif he thá "—	" If he then "—

The second leaf contains the following, belonging to the

---

[108] This seems to be a proverbial expression,—" the landmark removed " beyond the boundary,"—applied to Waldhere's aggressive conflicts.

[109] Mr. Thorpe, Codex Exoniensis, translates æt-stealle " refection-" place;" but the context, speaking of S. Guthlac's warfare with the powers of darkness, shows that it means rather the standard, or the spot where the standard was planted for battle:—

" him to æt-stealle	" for his standard
" ærest arærde	" first reared
" Cristes róde."	" Christ's rood."

sequel of the story, but not immediately connected with the above:—

—" (beado-me)ce bæteran,	—" battlesword better,
" búton thám ánum,	" save that one,
" thá ic eác hafa on stán-fate	" which I eke in the stone-chest
	" have
" stille gehíded.	" stilly hidden.
" Ic wát thæt ic thóhte,	" I knew that I thought,
" Theodríc Widian	" Theodric with Widia
" selfum on-stódon,	" himself stood forward,
" and eác sinc micel	" and eke much treasure
" máthma mid thí mece,	" of ornaments with the sword,
" monig othres mid him	" many another with them
" golde gegirwan.	" to grace with gold.
" Iu leán genám,	" Of old he received reward
" thæs the hine of nearwum	" because that him out of prison
"Níthhádes mæg,	" Nithhad's kinsman,
" Welandes bearn,	" Weland's son,
" Widia út-for-lét;	" Widia delivered;
" thurh fifela gefeald	" through the monster's territory
" forth onette.	" forth proceeded.
" Waldere mathelode,	" Waldere spake,
" wiga ellen-róf	" (the mighty warrior
" hæfde him on handa	" had in his hand
" Hilde frore,	" Hild's icicle,
" gúth-billa grípe,	" the gripe of war-bills),
" gyddode wordum.	" spake in words.
" Hwæt, thú húru wéndest,	" Lo! thou at least thoughtest,
" wine Burgenda,	" friend of the Burgends,
" thæt me Hagenan hand	" that me the hand of Hagena
" hilde gefremede,	" finished in conflict,
" and getwæmde féthe	" and divided the path
" Wigges féta.[110]	" of Wig's feet.
" Gyf thú dyrre, æt thus [111]	" If thou dare, in such combat,
" heatho,	
" werigan háre byrnan,	" wear thy white byrnie,

---

[110] Mr. Stephens suggests that *feta* is an archaic form of the dative singular. I regard it as the genitive plural, for *fóta*.

[111] Mr. Stephens reads *Thurs heatho*, " Thor's conflict."

" standath me hér on eaxelum	" here rests on my shoulder
" Ælfheres láf,	" Ælfhere's legacy,
" gód and geap neb,	" good and curve-pointed,
" golde geweorthod,	" adorned with gold,
" ealles unscende,	" altogether unshent,
" æthelinges reáf,	" the spoil of the ætheling,
" (halwend) to habbanne	" wholesome to have,
" thonne hád wereth	" when the hood defendeth
" feorh-hord feóndum.	" the life-hoard from foes.
" He bíth fáh with me,	" He shares feud with me
" thonne unmægas	" when strangers
" eft onginnath,	" again begin,
" mecum gemétath,	" meet me with swords,
" swá ge me dydon.	" as ye did me.
" Theah mæg sige syllan,	" Yet may victory give,
" se the symle býth	" He who is always
" recon and ræd-fest	" just and constant
" rýhta gehwilces.	" of each one's rights.
" Se the him to thám Hálgan	" He who himself to the Holy
" helpe gelifeth,	" trusteth for help,
" to Gode gióce,	" to God for aid,
" he thær gearo findeth.	" he there readily findeth it.
" Gif thá earnunga	" If then of retribution
" ǽr gethenceth,	" one think beforehand,
" thonne mtoten[112] wlance	" then might we proud ones
" welan britnian,	" enjoy our wealth,
" ǽhtum wealdan.	" rule our possessions.
" Thæt is "—	" That is "—

These precious fragments, with the Traveller's notices of Guthhere, Gislhere, Ætla, and Eormanric, as his cotemporaries, lead us to the most interesting part of our inquiry, the relation of these poems to the grand cycle of Teutonic romance. These fragments evidently belong to an Anglo-Saxon version of the story, which Gerald of Fleury paraphrased in Latin hexameters, in the tenth century,—a version which represented the original more faithfully and in a purer form

---

[112] Sic for *móton*.

than the said paraphrase does. To be assured that it was more faithful, we need but advert to the circumstance, that, in these fragments, Guthhere is represented as a Burgundian prince, "friend of the Burgends," which he really was, and, in the Latin poem, he is uniformly represented as a king of the Franks. Similar licence, doubtless, has been taken by the poet, when he assigns to Herric the kingdom of Burgundy, and to Alfer that of Aquitaine; yet he may, perhaps, have given us the substance of the story correctly, and his poem enables us to understand, to a certain extent, these precious relics of the Anglo-Saxon saga.

He tells us, that Attila invaded the territory of the Franks, and received from king Gibic, as a hostage, a young noble called Hagen, because Gibic's son Gunther was too young to be taken from his mother; that then he proceeded against Burgundy and Aquitaine, and received, as hostages, from Herric and Alfer, the sovereigns respectively of those territories, Hildigund the daughter of the former, and Walther the son of the latter. Hagen and Walther were educated at the court of Attila, and treated in every respect as his sons, and Hildigund, in like manner, was treated as a daughter by Attila's queen, Ospirn. In process of time, Hagen, having heard of the death of Gibic and the accession of Gunther, regarded himself as released from his engagements, and fled to his own country. Attila, fearing lest Walther should follow Hagen's example, offered him a wife and land; but Walther declined his offers, being secretly attached to Hildigund, who had been betrothed to him by her father, with his own father's consent, before they left their homes. He distinguished himself as the leader of Attila's army. One day, returning victorious from battle, he found Hildigund in the palace alone, embraced the opportunity of declaring his love, and made arrangements with her for their flight. They effected their escape accordingly, after having entertained Attila and his nobles at a feast, and made them drunk; and reached in safety the frontiers of Gunther's kingdom. There Walther was treacherously attacked by Gunther and Hagen, with their warriors, but he defeated them, pursued his way to his own country, and married Hildigund.

In Biterolf, Walther and Hildigund are said to have been present at a feast given by Gunther to Rudiger, the ambassador of Attila; and in the Wilkina saga, Walther, as the leader of the forces of Hermanaric, is the ally of Gunther in a war with Attila, and perishes in single combat, together with Dictlieb, his adversary.

Our fragments belong to that part of Waldere's saga, which spoke of the unprovoked attack made upon him by Guthhere and Hagena. In the first, Hildigund is the speaker, addressing the son of Ælfhere as "Ætla's van-warrior," (which he had recently been), reminding him of his valiant deeds, and assuring him of success, because Guthhere's attack was unjust. In the second, Guthhere and Waldhere are holding parley, prelusive to a combat, and the latter alludes to Hagena's attack upon him. As far, therefore, as they extend, these fragments are in accordance with the poem, except in the single instance which has been already referred to, and in this their superior accuracy is indisputable; but they contain also allusions to circumstances, on which the later sagas throw no light.

The theory that all these sagas are founded on Anglo-Saxon traditions, and that Eormanric and Ætla reigned in England, will be found to receive striking confirmation, from the names of places in the territories, which respectively owned their sway, and which, as indicated by these names, appear to be situated, relatively to each other, exactly as the sagas would lead us to infer that they were.

Discarding from the story of Eormanric, the circumstances which Jordanis relates of the great Hermanaric, and which there is no reason to believe are not correctly ascribed to him, we gather from the sagas the following outline of his history.

An extensive territory owned his sway, and many kings were subject to his authority. This accords with what Deor sings of him, and with Boece's statements, that he attacked the British king Constantine with a fleet, and that he made a league, which he faithfully kept, with the Picts and Scots; both which indicate that his dominions were not confined to Kent. We shall be able to form some idea of the extent of his kingdom, after we have noticed his connections, and the traces of their names which remain. Boece's notices of him are favourable to his character, and so also is the Traveller's; but the author of the poem of which the Traveller's Tale forms part, the author of Beowulf, Deor, and all the sagas, speak of him as a cruel tyrant. For the little that we know of him we are mainly indebted to the compositions of scalds, who were in the interests of his enemies.

The intrigues of Sifeca, a prince high in his confidence, and the influence which he exercised over Eormanric, are represented as having been the cause of his crimes, and of the hatred with which his memory was regarded. The Wilkina saga tells us that Eormanric had dishonoured Sifeca's wife during his absence, and that Sifeca, learning what had occurred, on his return, resolved on the destruction of Eormanric's race. At his suggestion, Eormanric undertook an expedition, for the purpose of exacting tribute from Oseric, king of the Russen; whilst they were away, he sent a message to a relative of his own, to put to death the king's son, Freotheric; and afterwards led Eormanric to believe that the murder had been contrived by Oseric. Other accounts say that Eormanric himself willed the murder; but it is easy to understand how the act of his favourite might be imputed to him, and the circumstantial narrative of this saga may possibly contain the truth.

The Herclings, Emerca and Fridla, sons of Theodhere, the brother of Eormanric, were the next victims of Sifeca's revenge. He found means to exasperate their uncle against them, and to instigate him to order them to be hanged.

He now began to sow enmity between Theodric, son of Theodmær, another of Eormanric's brothers. As the lay of Hildebrand imputes Theodric's misfortunes to Ohthere's jealousy, whilst these accounts implicate Sifeca only, they may be reconciled by the supposition, that Ohthere was Sifeca's instrument. Theodric however escaped, fled eastward into the land of the Huns, where Ætla received him kindly, and gave to him in marriage Herrad the niece of his queen Herche. Hildibrand accompanied him in his flight, leaving his bride and an infant son, afterwards called Heathobrand.

Theodric was early distinguished for his valour; he is said to have slain a giant, named Grim, and his wife, Hild; but in an encounter with another giant, named Sigenoth, the brother of Hild, he was not so fortunate; he was overpowered and cast into a dungeon, from which he was eventually delivered by Hildibrand. This seems to be the affair which is alluded to in the fragment of Waldhere's saga, where the deliverance is ascribed to Widia; if so, this is of course, as being earlier, more trustworthy.

Hildibrand was the son of Herebrand, and father of Heathobrand, and these are the Wylfings whom we have already had occasion to notice, and whose name we have found in Berkshire, at Wylfingaford. In Berkshire also, and in the neighbouring counties of Oxford, Wilts, Somerset, and Buckingham, we find traces of many others of the connections of Eormanric.

We have already noticed four places in Oxfordshire and Berkshire, which bear, or have borne, the name of Sifeca. Sevenhampton in Wiltshire, and Sevinestone,[113] now Simpson, in Buckinghamshire, may have been named after his son Seafona, (Sabene in the sagas), who is said on one occasion to have conducted the army of Eormanric against Ætla.

The name of Fridla the Hereling, whom, with his brother Emerca, the Traveller visited,[114] occurs at Frithelabyrig,[115] near Oxford, probably at Frilford not far distant, at Frideleshamor Frilsham, in Berkshire, and Frithelstock in Devonshire. Near Burford, in Oxfordshire, a stone pillar is mentioned in the records of the boundaries of Wychwood Forest, which has but lately disappeared, named Frethelestone. Marcham, the parish in which Frilford is situate, may bear the name of Emerca his brother, and Ecgerdeshel[116] that of Echeard, who is said to have been their guardian. That of Ohthere, whom the Traveller does not mention, frequently occurs; for instance, at Otterbourne, Hampshire, and Ottery, Otterford, and Otterhampton, Somersetshire. At Didmarton, in Gloucestershire, we find the name of Theodmær, and at Ditteridge in Wiltshire, and at Totteridge, (anciently Tedricesham[117]), that of his son Theodric. In the sagas, Theodric is usually called " of Bern," and this is generally Latinized

---

[113] Domesday.   [114] L. 226, 227.   [115] Cod. Diplom. 1216.
[116] Ibid. 556.   [117] Domesday.

"Verona," but in the "Genealogia Viperti comitis Groi-
"censis" it is called "Verdun." This is nearer to the truth;
for I have no doubt but that it was Farringdon, the ancient
name of which was Ferandun, as Henry of Huntingdon gives
it. Deor, however, leads us to understand that his residence
was Mæringaburg; and we have one distinct trace of the
Mærings in Berkshire, Mæringes thorn,[118] and another, about
which there can be very little doubt, Marridge hill, about
thirteen miles south of Farringdon, (Mæringa having been
changed into Marridge, as Wanating into Wantage, and
Torring, the name of a river in Devonshire, into Torridge).
Within a mile of the latter is Membury, and this name may
easily be believed to be a corruption of Mæringaburg.

Near Frilsham, in Berkshire, there is a circular fortress
called Grimsbury; and six miles distant from it is Ilsley,
(Hildleáh or Hildesleia in old charters). Near Burford in
Oxfordshire, is Signet, and near Long Wittenham in Berkshire, Sinodun hill, another ancient fortress. In these we
have the names of Theodric's antagonists, Grim, Hild, and
Sigenoth.

Scilling, who is mentioned by the Traveller,[119] in terms
which seem to indicate that he was Eormanric's scóp, has
given name to Scillinges bróc[120] near Long Wittenham.

Alverston, near Brading, in Wight, Alverstoke, near
Gosport, in Hampshire, and Ælfheres stapol[121] in Hampshire or Berkshire, bear the name of Ælfhere; and Wealderes
weg,[122] probably in Hampshire, and Walderes wil,[123] in
Wiltshire, that of his son Waldhere.

Herric who is mentioned in the Latin romance of Wald-

---

[118] Cod. Diplom. 1151. [119] L. 207. [120] Chron. Abingdon, I. 135.
[121] Cod. Diplom. 592. [122] Ibid. 774. [123] Ibid. 355.

here, is probably the Heathoric whom the Traveller visited.[124] It would appear that his territory was in the neighbourhood of Ælfhere's, and at Hatherley, and Hatherop, in Gloucestershire, (the latter near the borders of Oxfordshire and Wiltshire), and at Hatherden, in Hampshire, we have traces of his name.

Gifica's we have already found in Wiltshire.

Ludeger of Saxony, and Liudegart of Denmark, are represented in the Niebelungen lied as making war upon the Burgundians. Other sagas also mention them, but with some differences. In Biterolf they appear as Saxons, (except in one passage, where Ludeger is called king of Denmark), and allies of Gunter. In the Rabenschlacht, Liudegart is king of the Saxons, and Ludeger of the Misnians; and they are allies of Eormanric. In Dietrich's Flucht they are subjects, first of Ætla, then of Eormanric. Now we find these names very near together in Wiltshire, at Ludgershall and Liddiard, and we have besides another Ludgershall in Buckinghamshire, on the borders of Oxfordshire, and Ludegarstun,[125] in Gloucestershire, another Liddiard in Somersetshire, and Lidgeardes beorg,[126] in Berkshire, on the borders of Hampshire.

Two of the heroes of the sagas are honoured by the Traveller with a particular notice. At the conclusion of his story he says:—

"(I sought) Wudga and Hama. That was not the worst "of leagues, though I should always name them last. Full "oft the yelling spear flew, whining, from that band, on the "fierce nation, when the gold-decked chiefs, Wudga and "Hama, would avenge their men and women."[127]

Wudga is the Widia of the second fragment of Waldhere's

---

[124] Cod. Diplom. 233.   [125] Ibid. 654.   [126] Ibid. 1159.   [127] L. 250-262.

lay. He was the son of Weland, by Beadohild; received from his father, amongst other knightly gear, the celebrated sword Miming; and, thus equipped, challenged Theodric to fight, and would have killed him but for the intervention of Hildebrand. Eventually, however, after a successful career, he fell by Theodric's hand.

Hama also left his home, to seek his fortune as a warrior, and fought a duel with Theodric. Constantly associated in all his warlike enterprises with Wudga, he plays a conspicuous part in the sagas of Eormanric and Theodric. Beckhild, a sister of Brunhild, is named as his wife. Enmity arising between him and Sifeca, he left the court of Eormanric, lived a long time in solitude, and then entered a monastery. He quitted it, however, on Theodric's return to his paternal dominions, and resumed his warlike career.

Of these latter circumstances the author of Beowulf has something to tell us. Speaking of a collar, which Wealhtheow gave to Beowulf, he says:—

" I heard of no better in the hoard-treasures of heroes
" under heaven, since Hama bore away to Herebyrhte-byrig
" the collar of the Brosings, the jewel and its casket. He fell
" into the treacherous enmity of Eormanric, chose the æternal
" counsel." [128]

" Choosing the æternal counsel" seems to be well explained by the statement, that he lived in solitude for a time, and then entered a monastery, circumstances not at all improbable, since Boece says that Eormanric allowed Christianity to be preached amongst his subjects, though not himself a Christian. The enmity, which is described in the Sagas to Sifeca, and in Beowulf to Eormanric, was probably instigated by Sifeca, like the rest of the crimes which are imputed to Eormanric.

---

[128] F. 156.

Of Widia there is one clear trace in Dorsetshire, on the borders of Hampshire, at Wychbury, anciently Widian-byrig;[129] and Havant in the same county, anciently Haman-funt,[130] as well as Southampton, " Portus Hamonis," are named after Hama. In this county too, and in Berkshire, and Gloucestershire, we have traces of Hama's wife, Beck-hild. Behhilde slóh[131] was in Hampshire; Bæhilde stoc[132] probably in Berkshire; Beaghildæ byrigels,[133] now Beckett, near Ashbury, in Berkshire, marked her tomb; and Bechilde treu[134] was probably in Gloucestershire.

I think there can be little doubt that the seat of Eorman-ric's kingdom was on the borders of Oxfordshire, Berkshire, Gloucestershire, and Wiltshire, and probably at Oxford; that his dominions extended considerably to the west of Kent, and might comprise Berkshire, Oxfordshire, Buckinghamshire, and parts of Wiltshire, Somersetshire, and Hampshire. They were, therefore, as the Traveller says, " east of Ongle," the kingdom of Offa; and Eormanric might well, with so exten-sive a territory, come into collision, as Boece informs us, with Constantine, king of the Britons. Our history and these sagas are by no means discordant; on the contrary, their statement, that he put all his sons to death, is perfectly con-sistent with the historical fact, that his successor was Æthel-berht, a son begotten in his old age, and only eight years old when he came to the throne, in A.D. 560.[135] The natural re-

---

[129] Cod. Diplom. 633.   [130] Ib. 624.   [131] Ib. 1054.
[132] Ib. 592.   [133] Ib. 1148.   [134] Ib. 387.

[135] Possibly the difference of five years, in the dates which the Saxon Chronicle and Bæda give for the accession of Æthelberht, may be thus explained; A.D. 560 is the date of Eormanric's death, A.D. 565 is the year in which Æthelberht was allowed to take the kingdom, for which

sult of a minority in such times would be, that Æthelberht would succeed to a greatly diminished territory. During the greater part of Eormanric's reign, and whilst he was at the height of his power, the West Saxons appear to have made no advances. The unchronicled reign of Creoda occupied a great part of this period, and his dominion, as well as that of Cyneric, was probably very limited. From the conquest of Wight, at any rate, in A.D. 510, we hear nothing of their wars for forty years. In A.D. 551, and 555, towards the close of Eormanric's reign, they come under our notice again, engaged in repelling the advances of the Britons in Wiltshire; and the narratives of Cutha's and Ceawlin's campaigns, in A.D. 571 and 577, show that the Britons were then in possession of Buckinghamshire, Oxfordshire, and Gloucestershire. The Britons on the one hand, and the West Saxons on the other, may have availed themselves of this minority to encroach on Eormanric's territory, and Æthelberht's invasion of Wessex in A.D. 568, at the age of sixteen, may have been merely an effort on his part for the recovery of his hereditary rights.

Let us now turn to Ætla, and his connections. Oseric, son of Hertnit, is said to have been a king of the Russen in the North. He sent an embassy to Melias, king of the Huns, requesting the hand of his daughter, Oda, in marriage. Melias put the messenger in prison, whereupon Oseric made an expedition into the land of the Huns, and succeeded in carrying her off. Ætla is said to have abandoned his paternal dominions, and conquered Hunenland. He sought in mar-

---

his age disqualified him when his father died; a parallel to the case of Hygelac and Heardred.

riage Herche, the daughter of Oseric; was refused, but succeeded in obtaining her by a stratagem of the Markgrave Rudiger. Thenceforward he was the enemy of Oseric; and later, accompanied by Theodric, who assisted him in all his wars, he invaded the territory of Waldemar, Oseric's brother, defeated him with great slaughter, and conquered Russland.

Oseric has been already noticed as a tributary of Eormanric. His subjects were probably the Wrosnas of whom the Traveller speaks; we have found them in Lancashire, and there also we find the name of Waldemar, his brother, at Walmersley near Bury, and Walmersley near Bolton. Melias is very probably Mægla, or Melwas, who came to Britain with his father Port, reigned in Somersetshire, and on one occasion was opposed to Arthur. It is not said of what race he was; but the earlier Melga, or Melwas, appears to have been a king of the Huns, so that this was probably a Hunnish name; and in the district where he and his father landed, we find a single trace of another, Froila, at Froyle. The sagas speaks of a change of territory on the part of Ætla, and as we have noticed his name, as well as that of his enemy, Wulfhere, in Warwickshire, and in Norfolk, perhaps Wulfhere attacked him in the former, and was afterwards attacked and defeated by him in the latter. The war, of which the Traveller was a witness, resulted in what the sagas call Ætla's conquest of Hunenland, and he was established there, in Norfolk, at the time of which the sagas speak. In Warwickshire and Leicestershire, as well as in Norfolk and Suffolk, we find traces of persons who are connected with his history.

The name most worthy of remark, is that of Herche, who

is said, in many of the sagas, to have been Ætla's queen. It is so similar to Kerka, which Priscus gives as the name of the historic Attila's queen, that it might be regarded as borrowed by the sagas from his history; but the Latin romance of Waldhere calls her Ospirn, which corresponds in its initial element to that of her father Oseric,[136] and may represent her original name. Herche, then, may have been given to her after her marriage with Ætla, in memory of the queen of his earlier namesake; and it is remarkable that two places in England should have borne her name, both in the district where Ætla reigned, Herkeham,[137] in Norfolk, and Herchestede[137] in Suffolk. Three miles from Attleborough in Warwickshire, Oserry, now Erdsbury, may have been named after her father. In Gudrun's lied a Hunnish princess, Herborg, is mentioned; we find her name at Harborough, anciently Hereburge byrig,[138] nine miles from Attleborough. Hageneford,[139] now Hainford, in Norfolk, Yelvertoft in Northamptonshire, on the borders of Warwickshire and Leicestershire, Yelverton in Norfolk, and Walberswick in Suffolk, present traces of Hagen, Gelfrat, and Walber, who are mentioned in the sagas in connection with Ætla.

The Edda and the German sagas agree in saying, that Ætla married the daughter of Gifica, king of the Burgundians, but in the former she is named Gudrun, in the latter Chriemhild. The authority of the Edda, as being earlier, and likely to have preserved these traditions in a less corrupted form, is preferable; the sagas appear to have sub-

---

[136] It is almost needless to remark that the Anglo-Saxons affected similarity of names in their families.
[137] Domesday.   [138] Cod. Diplom. 710, 1298.   [139] Ib. 1270.

stituted for the name of Gudrun, that of her mother Crimhild, the wife of Gifica. At the time of her marriage with Ætla, Theodric and Irminfrid king of Thuringia were at his court. After seven years, plotting revenge against Hagen, the murderer of her first husband, Sigefrid, she invited her brother Guthhere to visit her. He accepted the invitation, and went, accompanied by her other brothers Gernot and Gislhere, as well as by Hagen, Dankwart, and Volkart, and a numerous following; for Hagen, who had been invited by name, and had reason to dread the vengeance of the queen, suspected treachery. The Niebelungen lied describes their journey, and its description is in perfect accordance with what we have supposed to be the relative positions of the territories of Guthhere and Ætla, and with the local nomenclature of the districts, through which the Burgundians must have passed, on their way to Attleborough.

Soon after they had crossed the frontier of their own kingdom, on account of an outrage committed by Hagen, they were attacked by a party of Huns, commanded by the brothers Gelfrat and Elsa, but repulsed them, and slew Gelfrat. They met with a kind reception in the territory of Rudiger, with whom they sojourned some time, and who gave to Gislhere his daughter-in-law in marriage. Thence they pursued their journey to the court of Ætla.

The district in which the Burgundian brothers Gunter, Gernot, and Gislhere resided, is indicated by the names of Gunnersbury and Isleworth in Middlesex. The prince with whom they sojourned on their way, is called Rodolf, as well as Rodingeir, in the Wilkina saga; the former probably his personal name, the latter one derived from that of his people, whose settlements we recognize in the Rodings, in Essex;

and in the neighbourhood of one of these Rodings, the parishes of Garnet, Great and Little, bear the name of one of the Burgundian princes. Thus we have a clear indication of the route they took, the old Suffolk way, through Essex; and in this county, the name of Elsa, who was visited by the Traveller,[140] occurs at Elsenham. Thus the kingdom of Ætla appears to be as distinctly localized as that of Eormanric, and consistently with the statement in the Lay of Hildebrand, that Theodric fled *eastward* from his own home to the court of Ætla.

To account for the presence of Irminfrid of Thuringia at the court of Ætla, we must turn to his history. He was married to Amalaberga, the niece of Theoderic king of the Ostrogoths, and at her instigation made war upon his brother Baderic, assisted by the forces of Theoderic king of the Franks, whose alliance he had secured, by a promise of half Baderic's territory. Baderic was defeated and slain, but Irminfrid would not fulfil his promise, so Theoderic, and his brother Chlothachari, invaded Thuringia, and put him to flight. In this war, Theoderic was assisted by Sweves, Saxons, and Bavarians; and although we know that Sweves, as well as Saxons, were settled in Britain at this time, we should not have known that Theoderic's allies came from Britain, but for the following very important passage, in the " Translatio Sancti Alexandri:"[141]—

---

[140] L. 235.

[141] " Saxonum gens, sicut tradit antiquitas, ab Anglis Britanniæ in-
" colis egressa, per Oceanum navigans, Germaniæ litoribus, studio ac
" necessitate quærendarum sedium, appulsa est in loco qui vocatur Ha-
" duloha, eo tempore quo Thiotricus rex Francorum, contra Irminfridum
" generum suum, ducem Thuringorum, dimicans, terram eorum ferro
" vastavit et igne. Et cum jam duobus præliis, ancipiti pugnâ incer-

" The race of the Saxons, as old tradition tells, emigrating
" from the Angles, the inhabitants of Britain, crossing the
" ocean with the desire, and under the necessity, of seeking
" settlements, arrived at the place which is called Haduloha,
" at the time when Thiotric, king of the Franks, warring
" against Irminfrid his son-in-law, the chief of the Thurin-
" gians, wasted their territory with fire and sword. And
" when they had fought in two battles with doubtful success,
" but with miserable slaughter of their people, Thiotric, dis-
" appointed in his hope of victory, sent messengers to the
" Saxons, whose leader was Hadugoto. For he had heard
" the cause of their coming, and, having promised them set-
" tlements, engaged them to assist him; with the aid of these,
" fighting bravely as if it had been for liberty and their
" country, he overcame his enemies, and, according to his
" promise, gave their territory to the victors, the natives be-
" ing wasted, and almost exterminated. They, dividing the
" land by lot, since many of them had fallen in the fight, and
" they could not occupy it all, on account of their small
" number, let out a part of it, and especially that which is to
" the east, to farmers, to be held on rent, but occupied the
" rest themselves."

" tâque victoriâ, miserabili suorum cæde decertassent, Thiotricus, spe
" vincendi frustratus, misit legatos ad Saxones, quorum dux erat Hadu-
" goto. Audivit enim causam adventus eorum, promissisque pro vic-
" toriâ habitandi sedibus, conduxit eos in adjutorium; quibus secum
" quasi jam pro libertate et patriâ fortiter dimicantibus superavit adver-
" sarios; vastatisque indigenis et ad internitionem pene deletis, terram
" eorum juxta pollicitationem victoribus delegavit. Qui eam sorte divi-
" dentes, cum multi ex eis in bello cecidissent, et pro raritate eorum
" tota ab eis occupari non potuit, partem illius, et eam quæ maxime
" respicit ad orientem, colonis tradebant, singuli pro sorte sua, sub tri-
" buto exercendam. Cætera vero loca ipsi possidebant." Pertz, ii. 674.

Goldast[142] has published an ancient document, which furnishes us with a distinct narrative of these events. Under a king named Rudolf, it is said, a multitude of Sweves were compelled by scarcity to seek settlements abroad, equipped a fleet, crossed the sea, landed at Schleswig, and plundered Denmark so successfully, that they were enabled to mount twenty thousand of their number on the horses they had stolen. Then, partly mounted, and partly on foot, they crossed the Elbe, and occupied the neighbouring districts. Theoderic, fearing lest they should make a league with Irminfrid, with whom he was then at war, hastened to attach them to his own interests, by promising to cede to them certain territories; and the mounted Sweves immediately joined his army, the rest remaining in their tents. Irminfrid attacked them, but was compelled to retreat behind the river Unstrut. For three days the Thuringians held one bank of the river, and the Franks and Sweves the other; until the former, despairing of success, sent Iring, Irminfrid's chief counsellor, to treat with Theoderic. A treaty of peace was at length arranged, the basis of which was, that the Thuringians should continue to hold their own territories, but as vassals of Theoderic. A Sweve who was informed of this by a Thuringian, carried the intelligence of it to his people, and they, fearing that Theoderic would break his engagements with them, and unite with Irminfrid to drive them out of the country, crossed the river in the night, and attacked the Thuringian camp with such fury, that five hundred only, with Irminfrid, escaped, and fled to Attila, king of the Huns. Then the Sweves were enabled to occupy without opposition the district watered by the river Unstrut.

---

[142] Rerum Suevicarum Scriptores.

These two narratives evidently relate to the same events, although the immigrants are called Saxons[143] in the one, and Sweves in the other. Each informs us, that necessity compelled them to seek a new home, that they were engaged by Theoderic to assist him in his war with Irminfrid, that they vanquished the Thuringians, and took possession of their country. One tells us the name of their leader, and that of the district in which they were encamped, Hadeln at the mouth of the Elbe; the other indicates the scene of the war, and the districts in which they were settled, in the interior of Saxony. Now it is remarkable, that the name of the king of these people in their native land is precisely that which is given in the Wilkina saga to Ætla's ally, Rodolf; his people, the Rodings, were neighbours of the Angles and Sweves from the earliest times, and of the Sweves we have found traces in Norfolk and Cambridgeshire. Irminfrid's protector cannot of course have been the historic Attila, who died seventy years before; we may therefore accept the probability, which so many circumstances combine to raise almost to certainty, that he was another of the name who reigned in Norfolk, cotemporary with Eormanric of Kent, and therefore with Irminfrid himself; and that in this theory we have found the key, to the right understanding and appreciation of these sagas.

Gregory of Tours says,[144] that Irminfrid perished by a fall

---

[143] If they came from England it would be natural to call them Angles or Saxons, even though they were really Sweves; so that there is no contradiction here. The great body of the nation of the Sweves at this time was settled in Spain, so that it is the more probable, that these belonged to tribes who had become detached from the nation.

[144] III. 8.

from the walls of a city, whilst he was conversing with Theoderic; but in the Niebelungen lied it is said, that he fell into the hands of Volkart and was slain. It is not my object to vindicate the details of sagas, in which ancient traditions are presented to us in such a corrupted form, as they are in this and others; yet I think that these two accounts may be reconciled, by supposing that Gregory found the name of Theoderic in the tradition which he records, and that he assumed him to have been the king of the Franks, instead of Theoderic, the ally of Ætla, with whom Irminfrid was associated in the war. This conjecture removes the improbability which appears in Gregory's story, that Irminfrid should have accepted an invitation from one who was his deadly foe, and whose character for treachery was so well known. The different versions, of the story of the Saxon settlement in Thuringia, supply an instructive example, of the way in which persons of the same name have been mistaken one for another, not only in the sagas, but in documents like these, of a more strictly historic character. Irminfrid's wife was the niece of Theoderic the Ostrogoth, as Jordanis and Gregory of Tours relate; yet in one of the above-cited narratives he is called the son-in-law, and in the other the brother-in-law of Theoderic the Frank.

The date of this event appears to have been about A.D. 528, and we cannot but remark the similarity of the circumstances, of Hadugot's settlement in Thuringia, and those of Henegest's coming to Britain, just a century earlier.

The Traveller's journey must have been some years previous to this date, for he speaks of Ætla as engaged in a contest with Wulfhere and Wyrmhere, of whom the sagas knew nothing, and of Emerca and Fridla as still living. It was therefore, as I have said, early in the reign of Eormanric, and of Theoderic the Frank; so that between its date and that of Eormanric's death, there is ample room for Theoderic's thirty years' exile, and for the tragedies, which form the subject of the sagas, and were being enacted at the time of the great emigration from England to France, of which Hadugot's was probably one instalment.

England, then, was the country of the Traveller's origin, and of the greater part at least of his wanderings. Setting out from the territories of his feudal lord, Eadgils, in Cheshire or North Staffordshire, he traversed the midland districts, and spent a considerable time in what is now Oxfordshire and Berkshire. In the midland counties, we have found vestiges of many of the princes and peoples whom he mentions; in Berkshire, and the adjacent counties, traces of the connections of Eormanric, and not only of those whom he names, but of others who are celebrated in the sagas; in Middlesex, the names of the Burgundian princes, whose course we have been enabled to follow, through Essex and Suffolk, to the kingdom of Ætla. I am satisfied that this Tale of the Traveller relates the history of real wanderings; else we should have had allusions to events of a later time,— the exile of Theoderic for instance, and the crimes of Eormanric,—of which the author of the poem, of which this Tale formed a part, was not ignorant, but of which the Traveller himself says nothing. Those to which he does allude, Offa's war with Alewih, and Hrothgar's defence of Heorote, must have occurred within his own recollection; and it is evident, that he speaks of the heroes of the Teutonic sagas, at a period some years earlier, than that to which the incidents related in these sagas must be referred. Thus he is an invaluable auxiliary, enabling us to claim for those sagas an English origin; to vindicate for them, however corrupted, a foundation in fact; to glean therefrom an outline of the history of our country during the earlier part of the sixth century; and, with their aid, to supply some particulars of the innumerable wars, and the names of some of the chieftains, otherwise unnamed, of which and of whom Henry of Huntingdon speaks, in his brief summary of the history of this eventful period.

At a later time, when the Traveller's cotemporaries, Eormanric and Theoderic, had passed away, the Scóp Deor lived, within the limits of their territories, where their names, and those of Weland and Beadohild, Geat and Mæthhild, were familiar in men's mouths as household words.

The Traveller's Tale, with the introductory lines, formed part of an epic poem, from which perhaps, had it been preserved to us, we should have learned more of his history. Yet, although the loss of it is much to be regretted, I think we have sufficient evidence, whereon to found a probable conjecture as to his identity. I can see no reason, of necessity or propriety, why " he must always name Wudga and Hama " last,"—characters who certainly were entitled to honourable mention among the first, for they were in no respect inferior to any of the heroes of their time,—unless he were himself Hama, and must name in connection with himself, his inseparable companion in arms. The circumstance of his having received a magnificent collar from Eormanric, seems to be that to which the author of Beowulf alludes, when he says, that " Hama carried away to Herebyrhte byrig, the " collar of the Brosings, the jewel and its casket;" and the statements with regard to Hama, that he enjoyed the favour of Eormanric for a time, but eventually incurred his displeasure, through the intrigues of Sifeca, will, (if we admit the identity of Hama with the Traveller), account for the different terms, in which the Traveller and the author of the poem which contains his Tale, speak of Eormanric.

In the district which I have supposed was occupied by the Myrgings, we have traces of both these chieftains. Wichnor and Hamstall Ridware are but a few miles south of Mackley and Marchington. Herberbery, or Harbury, in Warwickshire, may be the Herebyrhte-byrig, to which Hama retired, with the gift of Eormanric; Hampton Lucy, and Ham brook, are in its neighbourhood. Hama's collar was called the " Brosinga mene," because it had belonged to the Brosings, either before or after it came into Eormanric's possession. No trace of this family has been found out of England; but here one parish, Broseley, in Shropshire, is certainly named either from them or their progenitor, and so of course was their residence; and Brassington in Derbyshire perhaps was another.

The Lay of Hildibrand, to which occasional reference has been made in the foregoing pages, is interesting to philologists as an early monument of the German language; but those who may be disposed to admit the claims I have advanced, with regard to the heroes of the sagas, and the sagas which have perpetuated their renown, will regard it with feelings of greater interest still. It is the only relic, in a foreign dialect, of the grand Teutonic epos, that is worthy to be placed side by side with Beowulf, the Fight at Finnesham, the Lament of Deor, the Traveller's Tale, and the fragments of the Saga of Waldhere. Written on the first and last leaves of a MS. of the Books of Wisdom, of the ninth century, (in the Library at Cassel), it seems to have been preserved to us, as it were, fortuitously.

Theodric has returned, after thirty years of exile, to claim his paternal dominions, and the poet recounts to us the story of Hildibrand, his faithful companion, encountering his son Heathobrand in front of the two armies:—

" Ik gihorta that seggen,	" I heard say that,
" that sih urhettun ænon muotin,	" that challenged one another " to single combat,
" Hiltibraht enti Hathubrant,	" Hildibrand and Hathubrand,
" untar heriun tuem,	" in sight of the two armies,
" sunu-fatarungo;	" of the son and the father;
" iro saro rihtun,	" raised their weapons,
" garutun se iro gudhamun,	" prepared their war-coats,
" gurtun sih iro suert ana,	" girded on their swords,
" helidos ubar ringa,	" the heroes over rings,
" do sie to dero hiltu ritun.	" when they went to the fight.
" Hiltibraht gimahalta,	" Hildibrand spake,
" Heribrantes sunu;	" Heribrand's son;
" her uuas heroro man,	" he was the elder man,
" ferahes frotoro;[145]	" more prudent of soul;
" her fragen gistuont, fohem " uuortum,	" he stayed to inquire, in few " words,
" wer sin fater wari,	" who his father was,
" fireo in folche;	" of men in the nation;
" eddo welihhes cnuosles du " sis.[146]	" or of what race art thou. " If thou tellest me of one,
" Ibu du mi œnan sages,	
" ik mi de odre uuet.	" I know myself the other.
" Chind in chunincriche,	" Child in the kingdom,
" chud ist min al irmindeot.	" known to me is all the nation.
" Hadubraht gimahalta,	" Hathubrand spake,
" Hiltibrantes sunu;	" Hildibrand's son;
" Dat sagetun mi usere liuti,	" That told me our people,

---

[145] No alliteration. The Grimms suggest the transposition—
" her uuas frotoro man ferahes heroro."
[146] Here also the Grimms suggest the transposition—
" fireo in cnuosle eddo welihhes folches du sis."

THE LAY OF HILDIBRAND.

" alte anti frote,	" old and sage,
" dea er hina-warun,	" who long ago departed,
" dat Hiltibrant,	" that Hildibrand
" hætti min fater.	" my father was called.
" Ih heittu Hadubrant.	" I am called Hathubrand.
" Forn her ostar gihueit,	" Long ago he went eastward,
" floh her Otachres nid,	" fled from Otachar's enmity,
" hina miti Theotrihhe,	" hence with Theodric,
" enti sinero degano filu.	" and many of his thanes.
" Her furlaet in lante,	" He left in the land,
" luttila sitten	" sit a little
" prut in bure,	" bride in bower,
" barn unwahsan,	" a child ungrown,
" arbeolaosa heract.	" a destitute family.
" Ostar hina det,	" Eastward hence he went,
" sid Detrihhe	" after Theodric
" darba gistuontum,	" evils befel,
" fatereres mines.	" of my uncle.
" Dat uuas so friuntlaos man.	" That was so friendless a man.
" Her was Otachre	" He was to Otachar
" ummett-irri,	" very hostile,
" degano dechisto.	" most famous of thanes.
" unti Deotrichhe	" until Theodric
" darba gistontun.	" evils befel.
" Her was eo folches at ente.	" He was ever at the head of
	" the nation.
" Imo wuas eo feheta ti leop.	" Fighting was ever dear to him.
" Chud was her	" Known was he
" chonnem mannum.	" to brave men.
" Ni waniu ih iu lib habbe.	" I ween he lives not now.
" Wittu irmingot,	" Witness thou, mighty God!
" quad* Hiltibraht,	" quoth Hildibrand,
" obana ab heuane,	" above from heaven,
" dat du neo danahalt mit sus	" that thou in no wise with a
" sippan man	" man so related
" dinc ni gileitos.	" hast sanctioned conflict.
" Want her do ar arme	" Wound he then from his arm
" wuntane bouga,	" the circling bracelet,

---

* From this word to *inwit*, the writing is by another hand.

" cheisuringu gitan,	" imperially formed,
" so imo seder chuning gap,	" as once the king gave to him,
" Huneo truhtin.	" the lord of the Huns.
" Dat ih dir it nu bi huldi gibu.	" That I give thee now for
	" good will.
" Hadubraht gimalta,	" Hathubran spake,
" Hiltibrantes sunu ;	" Hildibran's son ;
" Mit geru scal man	" With spear shall one
" geba infahan,	" take the gift,
" ort widar orte.	" point to point.
" Du bist dir alter Hun	" Thou art to thyself, old Hun,
" ummet-spaher ;	" very crafty ;
" spenis mih mit dinem wuortun.	" thou beguilest me with thy
	" words.
" Wilihuh di nu	" I will now thee
" speru werpan.	" strike with the spear.
" Pist al so gialtet man,	" Aged man as thou art,
" so du ewin inwit* fortos.	" so thou hast always practised
	" deceit.
" Dat sagetun mi	" That said to me
" sæo-lidante,	" sea-farers,
" westar ubar Wentil-sæo,	" westward over the Wendel-sea,
" dat inan wic furnam.	" that war took him away.
" Tot ist Hiltibrant,	" Dead is Hildibrand,
" Heribrantes suno.	" Heribrand's son.
" Hiltibrant gimahalta,	" Hildibrand spake,
" Heribrantes suno ;	" Heribrand's son ;
" Wela gisihu ih,	" Well do I see,
" in dinem hrustim,[147]	" in thy armour,
" dat du habes	" that thou hast
" heine herron goten ;	" no good lord ;
" dat du noh bi desemo riche,	" that thou yet in this kingdom,
" reccheo ni wurti.	" art not a hero.
" Welaga nu, waltant got,	" Alas! now, mighty God!
" quad Hiltibrant,[148]	" quoth Hildibrand,
" we wurt skihit.	" how fate urges!

---

[147] The Grimms suggest *sitim*, "moribus," for *hrustim*, on account of the defect of alliteration.

[148] The Grimms suggest the transposition—
  " Welaga nu, quad Hiltibrant, waltant got."

" Ih wallota	" I wandered
" sumaro enti wintro	" summers and winters
" sehstic urlante,	" sixty abroad ;
" dar man mih eo scerita	" where man me ever destined
" in folc sceotantero.	" among the shooter's people.
" So man mir at burc ænigeru,	" So man me at any city,
" banun ni gifasta.	" has not bound as a murderer.
" Nu scal mih suasat chind	" Now shall my own child me
" suertu hauwan,	" hew with sword,
" breton mit sinu billiu,	" destroy with his bill,
" eddo ih imo ti banin werdan.	" or I be his murderer.
" Doh maht du nu aodlihho,	" Therefore mayest thou easily,
" ibu dir din ellen taoc,	" if thy strength avails thee,
" in sus heremo man	" from so old a man
" hrusti giwinnan,	" win armour,
" rauba bi hrahanen;	" spoils from his corpse;
" ibu du dar enic reht habes.	" if thou there shalt have any " right.
" Der si doh nu argosto, quad " Hiltibrant	" Be he then the basest, quoth " Hildibrand
" Ostarliuto,	" of Eastern people,
" der dir nu wiges warne,	" who shall now refuse thee the " fight,
" nu dih es so wel lustit.	" now it pleases thee so well.
" Gudea gimeinun,	" Good companions!
" niuse de motti,	" let the encounter determine,[149]
" wer dar sih dero hiutu hregilo	" who there to-day of these vests
" brumen muotti,	" may boast,
" erdo[150] desero brunnono	" or these byrnies
" bedero uualtan.	" both possess.
" Do lættun se ærist	" Then let they first
" asckim scritan,	" cut with their ash-spears,
" scarpen scurim,	" with sharp dints,
" dat in dem sciltim stont.	" that stood in the shields.
" Do stoptun to-samane ;	" Then stepped they together ;
" staimbort chludun ;	" their stone-axes resounded ;
" hewun harmlico	" they hewed harmfully

---

[149] This is the correspondent of *campus judicet*, " let the field decide," of the Anglian law.

[150] eddo.

" huitte scilti,	" the white shields,
" unti im iro lintun	" until their linden bucklers
" luttilo wurtun,	" became little,
" giwigan miti wabnum."	" to contend with weapons."[151]

Here unfortunately the MS. ends. For the result of the battle we must have recourse to the Wilkina saga, which, although it differs materially in the details of this story, may perhaps have preserved an outline of the tradition. There, at least, the unamiable temper which characterizes Heathobrand in this poem, is pourtrayed even more strongly.

The aged Hildibrand leaves Theodric's army, resolved to seek his son, meets, and recognizes him, by tokens which had been previously indicated to him. They encounter at first with spears, then dismount and continue the battle with their swords. Alebrand (Heathobrand) repeatedly demands the name of his antagonist, and Hildibrand in turn inquires if he be of Ylfing-(Wylfing)-race. This Alebrand denies, and immediately afterwards is disabled by a terrible blow, which cuts through his mail-shirt, and wounds his hip. He now pretends to surrender; but, as Hildibrand holds forth his hand to receive the proffered sword, Alebrand aims a treacherous blow at him, which, had it not been skilfully warded, would have severed his hand. Hildibrand remarks, " A wo-" man taught thee that stroke, not thy father;" then, after completely mastering him, asks, " Art thou my son Alebrand? " I am thy father Hildibrand." They embrace, and kiss each other, mount and ride to Bern. There is a happy meeting between Hildibrand and his wife. The next day Alebrand assembles the people, announces to them the ap-

---

[141] " Die beiden ältesten deutschen Gedichte," by the brothers Grimm, in 1812. W. Grimm, in 1829, published facsimiles of the MS.

proach of Theodric, and asks whether they will have him or Sifka for king. They declare their attachment to Theodric, and go forth to bid him welcome.

Here we take our leave of the sagas, and in the next chapter shall resume the chronicled history of the sixth century. Will no one undertake the publication and collation of the two versions of the saga of Ætla,—the Latin, in the Library of Corpus Christi College, Cambridge, and the French, in the Library of Sir Thomas Phillipps, Bart.?

CHAPTER IX.

The Annals of the Sixth Century.

A. D. 534.

YNERIC succeeded to the kingdom of the West-Saxons, and reigned twenty-six years, seventeen of which were passed without disturbance on the part of the Britons. His expedition on behalf of Burghard, against Wasing, must be referred to an early period of his reign.

A. D. 544. Wihtgar, his relative, died, and was buried in the neighbourhood of the town, which was named after him Wihtgares-byrig, now Carisbrook.

A. D. 547. Ida founded the kingdom of Bernicia.

— 551. "In the eighteenth year of his reign, Cyneric "fought against the Britons who had come with a very great "army to Salisbury. But he, having collected auxiliaries "from all quarters, met them most victoriously, and their "immense forces being routed, scattered them on either "hand, and put them to flight."[1]

---

[1] "Kinric rex, anno XVIII regni sui, pugnavit contra Britannos, qui "venerant cum magno exercitu usque ad Salesbirig. Ille autem, undique "congregatis auxiliis, occurrit eis invictissime, ingentibusque copiis fusis, "utrinque dispersit eos et in fugam convertit." HEN. HUNT.

This statement of Henry of Huntingdon shows that Wiltshire was in the hands of Cyneric, and that this was an invasion of his dominions on the part of the Britons.

A. D. 555. "Cyneric in the twenty-second year of his reign, and Ceaulin his son, fought again with the Britons. But it was fought thus:—The Britons, as it were to avenge the confusion of war which they had suffered about five years before, warriors being assembled, furnished with arms and strong in numbers, arrayed their ranks at Beranburi; and when they had set in order nine divisions, which number is most proper for war, to wit, three being placed in the front, and three in the centre, and three in the rear, and leaders being suitably appointed in those divisions, and the archers, and javelin-throwers, and cavalry, being disposed according to the system of the Romans, the Saxons, all collected together in one body, rushed upon them most boldly; and the standards being scattered and overthrown, and the spears broken, they carried on the affair with swords, until at the close of day the victory remained doubtful."[2]

The Saxon Chronicle merely notices the battle, and as there is no claim to victory for the Saxons, I suspect that

---

[2] "Kinric, XXII anno regni sui, et Ceaulin filius ejus, pugnarunt iterum contra Britannos. Sic autem pugnatum est: Britanni quasi vindicaturi confusionem belli, quam circa quinquennium pertulerant, congregatis viris bellicosis, armis et numero munitis, acies ordinaverunt apud Beranburi; cumque statuissent novem acies, qui numerus bello est aptissimus, tribus scilicet in fronte locatis, et tribus in medio, et tribus in fine, ducibusque in ipsis aciebus convenienter institutis, virisque sagittariis et telorum jaculatoribus equitibusque jure Romanorum dispositis, Saxones in eos, omnes in unâ acie conglomerati, audacissime irruerunt, vexillisque collisis et dejectis, fractisve lanceis, gladiis rem egerunt; donec, advesperascente die, victoria in dubio remansit." HEN. HUNT.

the result was favourable to the Britons; and that this was the battle of Harddnenwys, mentioned in the " Song of the " Ale," in which Urien of Rheged commanded the Britons. It began at Barbury hill, near Ogbourn S. George, in Wiltshire, and was continued and completed at Hardenhuish, fourteen miles to the westward. Four miles still further to the west is Slaughterford.

A.D. 558. Ælle became king of Deira, probably succeeding Beowulf.

The Cambrian genealogist says:—

" Then, in that time," (of Ida), " Dutigirn fought bravely " against the nation of the Angles. The Talhaern Talanguen " flourished in poetry, and Neirin, and Taliesin, and Bluch- " bard, and Cian, who is called Gueinchguant, flourished " together in British poetry. Mailcun, a great king, reigned " among the Britons, that is, in the region of Guenedotia; " for his great grandfather, that is, Cunedag, with his sons, " whose number was eight, had come previously from the " northern part, that is, from the region which is called " Manau Guotodin, one hundred and forty-six years before " that Mailcun reigned; and they expelled the Scots with " immense slaughter from those regions, and they never re- " turned again to dwell there."[3]

---

[3] " Tunc Dutigirn in illo tempore fortiter dimicabat contra gentem " Anglorum. Tunc Talhaern Talanguen" (vel " Cataguen " vel " Tat " Anguen") " in poemate claruit, et Neirin et Taliessin, et Bluchbard, et " Cian, qui vocatur Gueinchguant," (vel " Guenith Guant"), " simul in " uno tempore in poemate Brittannico claruerunt.

" Maileunus magnus rex apud Brittones regnabat, id est, in regione " Guenedotæ, quia atavus illius, id est, Cunedag cum filiis suis, quorum " numerus octo erat, venerat prius de parte sinistrali, id est, de regione " quæ vocatur Manau Guotodin, centum quadraginta sex annis antequam

Of Ida's antagonist Dutigirn, nothing more is known. If the flight of Cunedda took place, as I have supposed, in A. D. 410, Mailcun's accession must be dated A. D. 556. He is of course a different person from the king, whose death the Annals of Cambria record ten years after the battle of Camlann, the fifth ancestor of Cadwallo. He is noticed afterwards, as the leader of the forces of Gwynedd, in the battle of Ardderydd, and he fell in the battle of Cattraeth.

Many poems are ascribed to Taliesin; but they are of very doubtful authenticity, and even those which appear to have the best claim to be considered genuine, in their present form are not earlier than the twelfth century, and contain verses which there is great reason to believe are interpolations. These are devoted to the praises of Urien of Rheged, his son Owain, and Gwallawg ap Lleenawg.

One, which has been already quoted, mentions eight battles fought by Urien with the Angles, at Alcluyd, Inver, Cellawr Brewyn, Hireurur, Cadleu, Aberioed, Cludwein and Pencoed. One of the poems in praise of Gwallawg, notices his presence with Maelgwn at the last. Wlph was Urien's antagonist.

Another, descriptive of the battle of Gwenystrad, does not tell us who his opponents were, but it seems, from the sixth line, that they were Britons.

A third, the most interesting of the series, speaks of a battle fought from sunrise to sunset, at Argoed Llwyfain; of Flamdwyn advancing with his troops, in four divisions, extending from Argoed to Arfynyd; of his demanding host-

---

" Mailcun regnaret, et Scottos cum ingentissimâ clade expulerunt ab
" istis regionibus, et nusquam reversi sunt iterum ad habitandum."

ages and Owain refusing them; and it is intimated that Flamdwyn was slain, and his army entirely routed. An elegy on Owain says, that Flamdwyn fell by his hand.

Flamdwyn has been, without any warrant, identified with Ida. It is far more probable that he was Flaem or Flayn, who, with his brother Scardyng, is said to have been amongst the followers of a chieftain named Engle, in old traditions, which are preserved in the Chronicle of Robert of Brunne. Flamborough bears his name, and Scarborough is said to have been given to his brother.

We have no indication of the date of these conflicts of Urien with Wlph and Flamdwyn, but possibly they are those of which Henry of Huntingdon speaks, as anterior to Ida's establishment of the kingdom of Bernicia; and Engle and his nineteen sons may have accompanied him and his father.

A.D. 559. Adda, son of Ida, succeeded him in Bernicia.

After noticing the reigns of Ida's successors, the Cambrian genealogist continues:—

"Against them four kings Urbgen, and Riderchhen, and "Guallanc, and Morcant fought."⁴

Rhydderch Hen appears, from the Life of S. Kentigern, to have begun to reign in Strathclyde about A.D. 560. We shall have occasion to notice him more particularly in the sequel. Guallanc is Taliesin's Gwallawg.

A.D. 560. Ceawlin succeeded Cyneric in Wessex. Eormanric, king of Kent, died, leaving a son, Æthelberht, eight years of age, who in

---

⁴ "Contra illos* quatuor reges, Urbgen, et Riderch-hen, et Guallanc, "et Morcant dimicaverunt."

* "Illos" is the reading of Gale's and other MSS.; "illum" is certainly wrong.

A. D. 565. succeeded to the kingdom.

— 566. Clappa succeeded Adda in Bernicia.

— 568. " Ceawlin, in the ninth year of his reign, and
" his brother Cutha, very bold men, urged by various causes,
" fought against Æthelberht, who had invaded their king-
" dom with proud forces. Engaging in conflict at Wipan-
" dune, they slew two of his princes, Oslaf and Cnebba, and
" an innumerable multitude with them, in the shock of battle,
" and made king Æthelberht flee to Kent. That was the
" first battle which the kings of the Angles fought amongst
" themselves."[5]

Æthelweard says that Ceawlin and Cutha were the aggressors. I have already said that I regard this as an attempt on Æthelberht's part, at the age of sixteen, to recover his hereditary rights, which had been wrested from him during his minority. If, however, Æthelweard be right, it will appear that he still retained the extensive territories of his father. Wipandune, (Wibbandun, or Uubbandune,) is most probably Wembdon in Somersetshire. The assertion, that this was the first breaking out of war amongst the kings of the Angles, is at variance with Henry of Huntingdon's statement, before cited.

A. D. 571. Theodwulf succeeded Clappa in Bernicia.

" In Ceawlin's twelfth year, his brother Cutha fought with
" the Britons at Bedcanford, which is now called Bedford;

---

[5] " Ceaulin, anno nono regni ejus, et Cutha frater ejus, viri audacis-
" simi, causis variis compellentibus, pugnaverunt contra Aedelbert, qui
" in regnum eorum viribus superbis introierat. Ingressi vero prælium
" apud Wipandum, duos consules ejus, scilicet Oslaf et Cneban, et innu-
" meram multitudinem cum eis, bello fulminantes, ceciderunt, regemque
" Aedelbert usque ad Kent fugaverunt. Istud est primum bellum quod
" inter se reges Anglorum gesserunt." HEN. HUNT.

" fought and conquered, and took by force of arms four fort-
" resses, viz. Lienberig, and Aelesbury, and Benesintune,
" and Aegnesham; but Cutha, a great man, the brother of
" the king, died in the same year."⁶

For the first of these Gaimar gives Luitone, *i.e.* Leighton
in Buckinghamshire; the rest are Aylesbury in Buckinghamshire; Bensington, and Ensham, in Oxfordshire. The
Britons had evidently followed up their success at Hardenhuish, and recovered much of their lost territory. The scale
of victory appears to have turned at this time in favour of the
West-Saxons.

A.D. 572. Frithuwulf succeeded Theodwulf in Bernicia.

— 577. " Ceawlin and Cuthwine, his son, in the eigh-
" teenth year of his reign, fought against the Britons; for
" three of their kings, Commagil, and Candidan, and Farin-
" magil, arrayed their disciplined and splendid forces against
" them, according to the rules of war, at Deorham. So the
" battle was fought most vigorously, but the Lord Almighty
" gave the victory to his enemies, and cast off his own people
" who had foolishly offended him; and on that day the afore-
" said three kings of the Christians fell, and the rest were
" put to flight. But the Saxons, having become terrible to
" them, in the pursuit of them took three most excellent
" cities, Gloucester, Cirencester, and Bath."⁷

---

⁶ " Ceaulini anno XII pugnavit Cutha frater ejus cum Brittannis apud
" Bedeanfordam, quæ modo dicitur Bedeforda; pugnavit igitur et vicit,
" cepitque armorum effectu IIII castra munita, scilicet Lienberig, et
" Aelesbury, et Benesintune, et Aegnesham; sed Cutha, vir magnus,
" frater regis, eodem anno obiit." HEN. HUNT.

⁷ " Ceaulin et Cuthwine, filius ejus, anno XVIII regni ejus, pugnaverunt
" contra Brittannos. Tres autem reges eorum Commagil, et Candidan,
" et Farinmagil, acies in eos confertas et splendidas, prælii legibus dis-
" tinxerunt, apud Deorham. Bellatum est igitur robustissime; victoriam

The scene of this battle was Derham in Gloucestershire. Its result was the addition of Gloucestershire to the West-Saxon territories.

A.D. 579. Theodric, son of Ida, began to reign in Bernicia.

To this year must be referred a battle which the Annals of Cambria record:—

"CXXIX year. Battle of Arderit between the sons of "Elifer, and Guendoleu son of Keidiau, in which Guendoleu "fell. Merlin became mad."

The Life of Merlin tells us,[8] that Rodarch, king of the Cumbrians, was associated in this battle with Merlin, king of the Demetians, and Peredur, (the son of Elifer), king of the Venedotians. The king of Scotland is called Guennolous, and there can be no doubt of his identity with Cennaleph of the Pictish Chronicle, and Ceanalath, or Cendaeladh, of the Annals of Ulster and Tighearnach.

" vero dedit hostibus suis Dominus omnipotens, abjecitque suos qui vane
" offenderant eum; et ceciderunt die illa tres reges Christianorum præ-
" dicti, reliqui autem in fugam versi sunt. Saxones vero horribiles eis
" facti, inter sequendum eos, tres urbes excellentissimas sibi ceperunt,
" Gloucestre, et Cirecestre, et Badecestre." HEN. HUNT.

[8] "Contigit interea plures certamen habere
"Inter se regni proceres, belloque feroci
"Insontes populos devastavisse per urbes.
"Dux Venedotorum Peredurus bella gerebat
"Contra Guennoloum, Scotiæ qui regna regebat.
"Jamque dies aderat bello præfixa, ducesque
"Astabant campo, decertabantque catervæ
"Amborum pariter miserandâ cæde nuentes.
"Venerat ad bellum Merlinus cum Pereduro,
"Rex quoque Cumbrorum Rodarcus, sævus uterque;
"Cædunt obstantes invisis ensibus hostes,
"Tresque ducis fratres, fratrem per bella secuti,
"Usque rebellantes cædunt perimuntque phalanges.
"Inde per infestas cum tali munere turmas
"Acriter irruerant, subito cecidere perempti." L. 23-37.

The former record, under A.D. 557,—

"The flight before the son of Maelchon,"

and the latter, under A.D. 560, express the same event more fully,—

"The flight of the Albanachs before Bruidi son of Maelchon."

Bruide became king of the Picts in A.D. 556 or 557, and he reigned a year with Cennaleph his predecessor; so that it would seem that he drove him out of the kingdom in A.D. 558; and that, in A.D. 579, Cennaleph made an attempt to recover it, but was defeated and slain. The name of Bruide's father, Maelcon, satisfactorily accounts for the presence of the forces of Gwynedd in this battle, if, (as is very probable), he may be identified with Mailcun or Maelgwyn. Arthuret, in Cumberland, appears to represent Arderit (or Arderydd), the place where it was fought.

The Cambrian genealogist continues :[9]—

"Deodric fought bravely against that Urbgen with his "sons. In that time one while the enemy, another the "natives were vanquished, and he (Urbgen) shut them up "three days and three nights in the island Medcaut; and, "whilst he was in the expedition, he was murdered for envy, "through Morcant's instigation, because in him above all the "kings was the greatest valour in the prosecution of the "war."

The date of this event is limited by the reign of Theodric;

---

[9] "Deodric contra illum Urbgen cum filiis dimicabat fortiter. In illo "autem tempore aliquando hostes, nunc cives, vincebantur; et ipse con-"clusit eos tribus diebus et tribus noctibus in insulâ Medcaut, et dum "erat in expeditione jugulatus est, Morcanto destinante pro invidiâ, quia "in ipso præ omnibus regibus virtus maxima erat in instauratione belli."

it must therefore have been between those of the battles of Arderydd and Cattraeth, (in which latter Urien's son Owain was the commander), *i. e.* between A.D. 579 and 586.

A.D. 584. "Ceawlin, in the twenty-fifth year of his reign, "and Cuthwine, fought with the Britons at Fedhanlea. It "was fought fiercely and terribly on either side. Cuthwine, "overpowered by a great multitude, was vanquished and "slain. The Angles, therefore, were routed and put to "flight; nevertheless king Ceawlin, having reorganized his "army, when his people had abjured flight, at length over- "came the victors in battle, and pursuing the Britons, took "many regions and innumerable spoils."[10]

The accuracy of this statement of Henry of Huntingdon is remarkably verified by the other notices of this event. The Irish Annals mention this and two of the following battles, (dating each three years earlier than the Saxon Chronicle); and Fordun supplies important details, which enable us to understand clearly the nature of the struggle. The Annals of Ulster, under A.D. 581, record,—

"The battle of Manann in which Aedan, son of Gabhran, "was victor."

The Annals of Tighearnach call it "prælium Mannense."

Fordun tells us,[11] that Aidan, who was consecrated king of the Scots by S. Columba in A.D. 570, and reigned thirty-

---

[10] "Ceaulin, vigesimo quinto anno regni sui, et Cuthwine, pugnaverunt "cum Brittannis apud Fedhanlea. Pugnatum est autem perniciose et "horribiliter utrinque : Cuthwine gravi multitudine oppressus, prostratus "et occisus est. Victi sunt igitur Angli, et fugæ dati, rex tamen "Ceaulin, rursus reparato exercitu, cum fugam sui abjurassent, tandem "prælio victores vicit; persequensque Brittannos, regiones multas et in- "numerabilia spolia cepit." HEN. HUNT.

[11] III. 27.

five years, was victorious over the Picts and Saxons, whenever they invaded his dominions; but that he suffered defeat on two occasions, when he assumed the offensive; once, when his army was led by Brendin, king of Man, and once when he commanded in person. His narrative of the former defeat is as follows:—

"Malgo, king of the Britons, when he heard the fame of
"his valour, sent messages to him, beseeching him that, in
"remembrance of old alliance and friendship, he would not
"refuse to aid him against the wicked heathen nation.
"Readily giving ear to so just a request, in the fifteenth
"year of his reign, he sent Griffin his son, an illustrious
"soldier, and Brendin, king of Man, his nephew by his
"sister, with a powerful force. He would not, however,
"have committed to them the conduct of so great an affair,
"since he was wont with prudence, and often, to lead his
"army in person, and intended himself to have taken the
"command of this expedition, had not his princes, with wiser
"counsel, dissuaded him from his purpose. Immediately
"on their departure, the northern Britons join them, and
"thus united they direct their march towards Malgo, securely,
"as fearing no danger. But lo! suddenly, on the third day
"after they had passed Stanmore, they meet not unexpectedly
"with the troops of the Pagans, whom Ceulin, king of the
"West Saxons, commanded, in the place that is called Fethan-
"leg; where, when they had bravely contended for a great
"part of the day, Cutha the son of Ceulin was slain, with the
"whole of the first division which he commanded. The
"other divisions of the Pagans did not on that account
"abandon the field through fear, but took care to press on
"more valiantly, until, with cruel slaughter, they routed both

" our people and the Britons, who at first seemed to be gain-
" ing the victory."[12]

Boece mentions Malgo as the ally of Aidan, and Bruide, king of the Picts, as confederate with the Saxons, in this battle, but confounds it with a later one, in which Æthelfrith was Aidan's opponent.

Now it appears that the Britons and Scots gained the victory in the first instance, and put the Saxons to flight; and this was the battle of Mann or Manann, now Mondrum, in Cheshire. Then Ceawlin rallied his forces at Fedhanlea, now Fadley, a few miles from Mondrum, and gained the victory. Thus the Annals of Ulster mention only Aidan's victory, and pass over his subsequent defeat; Fordun records the defeat only; whilst Henry of Huntingdon gives us both sides of

---

[12] " Misit autem ei nuncios Malgo rex Britonum, cum suæ probitatis
" præconium audisset, obsecrans, ut posteræ confæderationis et amicitiæ
" non immemor, auxiliari sibi contra nefandæ nationis ethnicam gentem
" non recuset. At ille faciliter tam justæ petitionis aurem inclinans
" effectui, filium suum Griffinum militem egregium, atque Brendinum
" Euboniæ regulum, ex parte sororis nepotem, anno regni sui XV cum
" manu potenti destinavit. Non enim illis hac vice tanti curam com-
" misisset negotii, cum antea nihilominus exercituum prudenter soleret
" et sæpius ducatum gerere, quia dictam per se profectionem regere dis-
" posuit, si non saniori consilio primates diligentius ipsum a proposito re-
" vocassent. Illis mox cum exercitu proficiscentibus Britones associantur
" Boreales, et sic conjuncti simul quasi nihil timentes secure Malgonem
" adire contendunt. Sed ecce subito, die tertiâ postquam Moram trans-
" issent Lapideam, in paganorum turmas, non improvisi penitus incidunt,
" quibus præfuit West-Saxonum rex Ceulinus, loco qui Fethanleg appel-
" latur, ubi cum non parvo dici spatio fortiter certassent, Cutha, Ceulini
" filius, cum totâ quam ducebat acie primâ peremptus est. Nec tamen
" ob id paganorum acies reliquæ quicquam timentes ex campo recedere,
" quin et fortius instare curabant donec et nostros et Britones, qui bellum
" primo videbantur evincere, crudeli cæde terribiliter effugarent."
III. 28.

the affair, and chronicles not only the defeat, but a great victory which preceded it.

A.D. 586. Æthelric, son of Ida, succeeded Theodric in Bernicia. Theodric is possibly the Loegrian chieftain who fell on the fourth day of the battle of Cattraeth; and as the length of his reign coincides with the interval between it and the battle of Arderydd, his predecessor Frithuwulf may have fallen on that occasion.

The Annals of Cambria say:—

"CXXXVI year. Guurci and Peredur the sons of Elifer "die,"

And these appear to be the same as Gwaourdur and Peredur, who were killed on the third day of the battle. In this battle the Saxons,—under Bradwen or Bun, who is thought to have been the widow of Ida, and probably her sons, though their names are not given,—with the Picts, attacked the Britons of different provinces, assembled for an annual festival, and almost entirely destroyed them. Most of the British chiefs were slain, and amongst them Owain, son of Urien.

A Pictish leader, Dyvnwal Vrych, was slain by Owain in this battle. His name seems to have perplexed those who have hitherto written on this subject, as it is identical with that of Domhnall Brec, king of the Scots, in the seventh century. He is, however, equally a historical character. He is noticed as having invaded Brecknock, and having been afterwards defeated by Caradoc Vreichvras, one of the chiefs who fell in this battle.

A.D. 588. Æthelric, son of Adda, succeeded Ælle in Deira.

— 592. Frithuwald succeeded him.

"A battle was fought at Wodnesbeorh, that is, the hill of

" Woden, and no small slaughter being made, king Ceawlin
" in the thirty-third year of his reign was driven from the
" kingdom."[13]

I follow Florence of Worcester here, for his account is confirmed by Fordun, and Henry of Huntingdon has evidently made a slip when he says, that Ceawlin died in the thirtieth year of his reign, and that this battle was fought in the third year afterwards. Ceawlin was certainly the leader on one side in this battle, but there were Angles on the other, confederate with the Britons and Scots. The Annals of Ulster record it three years earlier:—

" The battle of Lethroidh won by Aedhan, son of Gabhran,"

And Fordun adds the details:—

" King Aidan, in the twenty-third year of his reign, (A. D.
" 592), being requested by the Britons, and their king Cad-
" wallo, to aid them against the aforesaid Ceulin, proceeded
" with his army to Chester, where the Britons had assembled,
" prepared to fight against him. He, when he had heard
" this, advanced to meet them prepared for war, and a severe
" battle being fought at Wodenysborth, Cealin, and Quichelm,
" and Crida, the leaders on Ceulin's side, and many of the
" warriors of his army, perished, and he, fleeing wounded,
" was immediately deprived of the kingdom."[14]

---

[13] " Pugnatum est in loco qui dicitur Wodnesbeorh, id est 'mons
" 'Wodeni,' et strage non modicâ factâ, rex Ceaulin, anno imperii sui
" xxxiii expulsus est regno." FLOR. WIGORN.

[14] " A Britonibus et suo rego Cadwallone, rex Aydanus regni sui xxiii
" contra prædictum Ceulinum regem de subsidio requisitus, ad Cestriam
" cum suo perrexit exercitu, quo Britones cum eo turmatim globati per
" acies adversus ipsum dimicaturi convenerant. Quibus et ipse cum hoc
" audisset, cum suis paratus ad bellum obvius incedit, et apud Wodenys-
" borth duro commisso prælio, duces de parte Ceulini, Cealinus, et Quich-

According to this statement, the notice of the deaths of Ceawlin, Cwichelm, and Crida, which is placed under the following year in the Saxon Chronicle, should be united to that of the battle. Ceawlin is a West-Saxon prince, a namesake of the king; Cwichelm bears the same name as the son of Cynegils, who died in A.D. 636; Crida is possibly the king of the Mercians, the son of Cynewald. William of Malmsbury's notice of Wodnesdic, in connection with this battle, and the name given to it in the Ulster Annals, (Lethroidh, probably Liddiard in Wiltshire), show that Wodnesbeorh is Wanborough in their neighbourhood; not Wednesbury in Staffordshire. Not far from it, " Cwichelmes hlǽw "[15] bears the name of one of the princes who fell there.

Ceolric usurped the kingdom of the West Saxons, and reigned five years. According to William of Malmsbury, Ceawlin died soon afterwards in exile.

The kingdom of the Mercians, which, as we have seen, had been independent for more than a century, begins now to appear in history. Pybba succeeded Creoda in this year; and, some years later, was succeeded by Ceorl, who was reigning in A.D. 605, when Eadwine, the son of Ælle, sought refuge at his court.

A.D. 593. Æthelfrith, who is called " the cruel,"[16] succeeded his father Æthelric in Bernicia.

A.D. 597. The memorable year of the arrival of S. Augustine.

Ceowulf succeeded Ceolric in Wessex. " He fought and

" elm, et Crida, copiæque bellatorum sui pene perierunt exercitus, sed
" et ipse vulneratus fugiens regno statim privatus est." III. 29.

[15] Cod. Diplom. 693, 1289.

[16] " Qui vocatur ferus." HEN. HUNT.

" contended incessantly with the Angles, or with the Welsh,
" or with the Scots, or with the Picts."

A.D. 598. Hussa succeeded Frithuwald in Deira.

— 603. " In the seventh year of king Ceolwulf, Edelfert
" the cruel king of the Northumbrians, brave and ambitious
" of glory more than all the kings of the Angles, wasted the
" nation of the Britons. Wherefore, stirred up by his suc-
" cesses, Ædan, king of the Scots who inhabit Britain, came
" against him with an immense and brave army, but escaped
" with a few, vanquished. For almost all his army was slain
" in the celebrated place which is called Degsastan; in which
" battle also Tedbald, the brother of Edelfrid, was killed with
" all the army which he led; nor from that time has any of
" the Scottish kings dared to come to battle against the
" nation of the Angles."[17]

The Annals of Ulster, as usual, record this battle three years earlier than the true date, under A.D. 599:—

" The battle of the Saxons in which Aedan was defeated,"

And those of Tighearnach notice:—

" The battle against the Saxons by Aedan, in which fell
" Eanfraich, brother of Etalfraich, by Maelumha son of
" Baedan, in which he (Etalfraich) was victor."

---

[17] " Ceolwulfi regis anno VII. Edelfert rex ferus Nordhumbrorum,
" fortis et gloriæ cupidus, plus omnibus Anglorum regibus, gentem vasta-
" bat Brittonum. Nemo in tribunis, nemo in regibus plures eorum
" terras, exterminatis vel subjugatis indigenis, aut tributarias genti An-
" glorum, aut habitabiles fecit. Unde motus ejus profectibus Ædan, rex
" Scottorum qui Brittanniam inhabitant, venit contra eum cum immenso
" ac forti exercitu; sed cum paucis victus aufugit. Siquidem in loco
" celeberrimo, qui dicitur Degsastan, omnis per ejus est cæsus exercitus;
" in quâ etiam pugnâ Tedbald, frater Edelfridi, cùm omni illo quem ipse
" ducebat exercitu peremptus est; neque ex eo tempore quisquam regum
" Scottorum adversus gentem Anglorum in prælium venire ausus est."
HEN. HUNT.

Fordun says, that in the thirty-third year of Aedan, A. D. 602, " it was agreed between him and the Britons, that at a
" set time, they should attack on either side, he on the north,
" they on the south, the Northumbrian people, whom Æthel-
" frid, a valiant and wise king, who had continually harassed
" the Britons and Scots, then governed. The king therefore,
" although advanced in age, expecting that they on their part
" would do what they had agreed by treaty, invaded the
" parts of Northumbria, the time of night coming on; and
" whilst his army daily was engaged in burning and plunder-
" ing, king Æthelfrid, coming one day, with a compact
" force, upon the Scots engaged in this kind of plundering
" through the villages and the fields, overcame them, but not
" without great slaughter of his own people.

"After the said war, Æthelfrid miserably wasted the
" nation of the Britons, and made many of their territories
" either tributary to the nation of the Angles, or occupied by
" them, the natives being exterminated."[18]

Hence Æthelfrith was known amongst the Britons by the epithet Flesaur, the " desolator."

---

[18] "Conventum est inter ipsum et Britones, populos Northumbrenses,
" quos tunc rex fortis viribus et prudens Æthelfridus rexit, qui Britones
" continuis et Scotos affecit injuriis, iste quidem ad Boream, illi siquidem
" ad Austrum, utrisque partibus impetere condicto subfirmatâ fide termino
" convenirent. Rex igitur, quamvis ætate grandævus, adveniente
" nocturno tempore, sperans eos ex adverso facturos quod pacto pepi-
" gerant, Northumbriæ partes invasit, et dum per dies singulos incendio
" suus vacaret et spoliis exercitus, una dierum dispersos hujusmodi præ-
" dando per villas et arva Scotos, rex Æthelfridus condenso superveniens
" agmine, non absque suorum magnâ cæde superavit. Post autem dictum
" bellum rex Æthelfridus gentem Britonum misere vastavit, pluresque
" terras eorum, exterminatis indigenis, aut genti Anglorum tributarios,
" aut habitabiles fecit." III. 30.

Boece gives the name of the battle-field Deglaston, which seems to be more correct than Bæda's Dægsastan. It is now Dalston, near Carlisle; and as Aidan was certainly in Æthelfrith's territory when he was attacked, Cumberland must have formed at this time, as it certainly did later, part of the kingdom of Bernicia.

In the Bodleian MS. of the Saxon Chronicle, it is said, that Hering, the son of Hussa, conducted Aidan's army into Æthelfrith's dominions.

I have given my reasons for supposing that Hussa reigned in Deira until A. D. 605, when it fell into the hands of Æthelfrith; and certainly, in this circumstance, we have a probable pretext for Æthelfrith's having invaded Deira, and annexed it to his own kingdom. I suspect that this Hering was no other than Hereric, the nephew of Eadwine, and the father of S. Hild. Æthelfrith's second wife was Ache, the sister of Eadwine, and their eldest son S. Oswald, who was thirty-seven years of age at the time of his death, must have been born in the very year of Æthelfrith's conquest of Deira. Hereric was in banishment at the court of Cerdic, king of the Britons of Elmet, in A. D. 614; and was poisoned there, doubtless by Æthelfrith's instigation. For we know that, at the same time, he was compassing, by similar means, the death of Eadwine. Eadwine invaded Elmet, and expelled Cerdic; and this must have been in or before A. D. 616; for in that year, the year before his victory over Æthelfrith, the Annals of Cambria place Cerdic's death. On obtaining possession of the throne of Northumbria, Eadwine banished his sister, with her children, and those of Æthelfrith's first wife, Bebbe. These circumstances seem to furnish a clue to Hereric's parentage and history; and to warrant the conjecture, that Ache, the daughter of Ælle, was the wife of Hussa, and the mother of Hereric, and afterwards became the wife of Æthelfrith; that Hereric, who had taken part with the Scots in A. D. 603, found shelter among the Britons until A. D. 615 or 616, when the fear of Æthelfrith caused Cerdic to put him to death; and that Eadwine invaded Cerdic's kingdom on this account.

A. D. 607. "Ceolwulf fought a very great battle against the South Saxons; in which either army suffered very severely; but the slaughter was more terrible on the South Saxon side."[19]

A. D. 611. Cynegils succeeded him. In the fourth year of his reign,

A. D. 614, he associated his son Cwichelm with himself in the kingdom, and they fought with the Britons at Beamdune (Bampton in Oxfordshire). At the very beginning of the fight, panic seized the Britons, and they fled precipitately, leaving two thousand and sixty-two dead upon the field.[20]

Boece says that Æthelfrith was confederate with Cynegils on this occasion, and he and Fordun represent Cadwallo as

---

[19] "Ceolwulfus inter multa bella contra multos facta, quæ causâ brevitatis prætermissa sunt, pugnam maximam habuit contra Sudsexas; in quâ uterque exercitus ineffabiliter contritus est. Clades tamen detestabilior contigit Sudsexis." HEN. HUNT.

[20] "Quarto autem regni sui anno, assumpsit secum filium suum Kichelmum in regnum, et inierunt bellum contra Brittannos apud Beandune. Cum igitur obviarent sibi acies terribiliter et pulcherrime, vexillis inclinatis, in ipsâ primâ collisione invasit horror Brittannos, timentesque aciem securium maximarum splendentium et framearum magnæ longitudinis, fugâ in principio, sero tamen, potiti sunt. Saxones igitur, sine detrimento sui victores, numeravere mortuos Brittannorum, et inventi sunt mortui duo millia et sexaginta duo." HEN. HUNT.

leader of the Britons. The latter says, that he went secretly, with few attendants, to seek the aid of Eugenius, (Eochadh Buidhe), king of the Scots; that, having received fair promises from him, he repaired to Ireland, and thence to Armorica, whence he returned immediately with a large army, placed at his disposal by king Salomon; and that he harassed the Saxons in many battles. Of these only the last is recorded, the famous battle of Chester; in which Æthelfrith, after having put to the sword a number of the monks of Bangor, (twelve hundred according to Bæda, two hundred according to the Brut), who had come to pray for the success of their countrymen, defeated the British army, but not without great loss on either side. Bæda and the Brut are agreed, that Brocmail, the governor of Chester, escaped by flight; but the latter says, that the slaughter of the monks occurred after the battle was fought, and the city taken; which seems more probable. Neither of these authorities supplies any indication of the date of the battle; except that the latter seems to fix A. D. 616, the year of the death of Æthelberht, king of Kent, as a limit, by saying that it was fought at his suggestion. However, it is recorded in the Annals of Cambria and Tighearnach, with particulars, which enable us to determine it with something like certainty. In the former we read:—

" CLXIX year. The battle of Cair Legion, and there fell
" Selim the son of Cinan. The rest of Jacob the son of
" Beli."

Another copy connects the deaths of these princes.

The Annals of Tighearnach say, under A. D. 613:—

" The battle of Cairelegion, where the holy men were
" slain, and Solon Mac Conian, king of the Britons, fell; and

" king Cetula fell there. Etalfraich was the victor, who
" afterwards immediately died."

The record of the death of Cadwallo, whose presence at the battle of Bampton Fordun mentions; reasonable time allowed for his journeys to Scotland, Ireland, and Armorica, his return, and some battles previous to this; the statement that Æthelfrith died immediately after this battle; and the fact, that the Annals of Tighearnach are four years too early in their notices of this series of events; concur to fix A. D. 617, the year in which Æthelfrith was slain by Rædwald, as the date of this battle. The Brut does not mention the death of Cadwallo, but, consistently with the statement that he fell in this battle, records, immediately afterwards, the election of another king Cadwan. Previous to this, however, Æthelfrith is said to have been defeated at Bangor, with the loss of ten thousand of his army, by Brochmail, Blederic, duke of Cornwall, Margaduc, king of Demetia, and Cadwan, and to have fled to his own dominions. Cadwan followed him, and passed the Humber, and a battle was on the point of being fought, when peace was made by the intercession of mutual friends, and Cadwan and Æthelfrith agreed each to allow the other to remain in undisturbed enjoyment of his territories.

The whole sequel in the Brut is disfigured with the grossest misstatements. Authentic materials may have formed the groundwork of the story, but these are unfortunately blended together in the most hopeless confusion. It is probably true that Æthelfrith discarded his first wife Bebbe, when he married Ache, but he was not the father of Eadwine. What is said of Cadwallo's being defeated, and visiting Scotland, Ireland, and Armorica, Fordun relates more truly under A.D. 614. Aidan, the king of the Scots, is said to have been killed by Cadwallo, after the battle of Hatfield; he really died in A.D. 605; and Cadwallo is here, and throughout the whole story, confounded with his later namesake, who fell in the battle of Heavenfield, A.D. 634; yet he is made to survive it, and,—by another confusion with Cadwaladr who fell a victim to the pestilence of A.D. 664-5,—is said to have died of sickness, after a reign of forty-eight years. Cadwaladr, in his turn, is confounded with the West-Saxon Cædwealh; and Ine, the successor of Cædwealh, and Ivar Vidfadme, his ally, are claimed as chiefs of the Britons; and, to conclude this extraordinary series of historical blunders, Offa, the king of the Mercians, is called Æthelstan by Layamon, (for it was he who renewed the tribute of Peter's pence, sixty-five years after it had been established by Ine).

What truth may be concealed under the story of Eadwine's having been educated at the court of Cadwan, I cannot divine. It cannot be true that Eadwine was born there, for he was two years old at the time of his father's death; and it is impossible that he could have been brought up in ignorance of the Christian faith, under the auspices of so religious a prince as Cadwan. He might indeed have sought refuge amongst the Britons, at the age of nineteen, in A.D. 605, and have formed an intimacy, as related, with Cadwallo; and the hostility, to which he fell a victim, may have originated in jealousy of the imperial state he affected, of which Bæda makes particular mention. These matters, however, must always remain involved in uncertainty. All that we really know of Eadwine's early years is, that at some period of his exile he must have taken refuge with Ceorl king of the Mercians, whose daughter he married; that the hostility of Æthelfrith pursued him from kingdom to kingdom; that Rædwald, king of the East Angles, eventually espoused his cause, and placed him on the throne of the united kingdoms of Deira and Bernicia, by his victory over Æthelfrith, in A.D. 617.

At the beginning of the seventh century, Anglo-Saxon history begins to assume a more distinct character. Eight kingdoms are established, and six of these,—Kent, Sussex, Wessex, and Mercia, founded in the fifth century, and Bernicia and Deira, in the sixth,—have a history more or less complete. The foundation of the kingdom of the East-Angles must have been about the beginning of the sixth century, and Wiwa was its first king, but his great grandson, Rædwald, is the first who figures in our annals; and Sleda, who married the sister of Æthelberht, is the first king of the East-Saxons whose name is recorded, although there is reason to believe that his great grandfather Bedca reigned in England. Henceforth, for more than a century, Venerable Bæda is our great historian, and although his immortal work leaves much to be desired with regard to the other kingdoms, the history of Northumbria, at least, (of which, during the fifth and sixth centuries, we already know more, than of the rest), is almost complete.

THE END.

CHISWICK PRESS:—PRINTED BY WHITTINGHAM AND WILKINS, TOOKS COURT, CHANCERY LANE.

Just Published.

ESSAYS ON ARCHÆOLOGICAL SUBJECTS,

AND ON VARIOUS QUESTIONS CONNECTED WITH THE HISTORY OF ART, SCIENCE, AND LITERATURE IN THE MIDDLE AGES.

BY THOMAS WRIGHT, M.A. F.S.A.

CORRESPONDING MEMBER OF THE INSTITUTE OF FRANCE, ETC.

Two vols. post 8vo. printed by Whittingham, *illustrated with* 120 *Engravings, cloth,* 16s.

CONTENTS.

1. On the Remains of a Primitive People in the South-East corner of Yorkshire.
2. On some ancient Barrows, or Tumuli, opened in East Yorkshire.
3. On some curious forms of Sepulchral Interment found in East Yorkshire.
4. Treago, and the large Tumulus at St. Weonard's.
5. On the Ethnology of South Britain at the period of the Extinction of the Roman Government in the Island.
6. On the Origin of the Welsh.
7. On Anglo-Saxon Antiquities, **with a particular reference to the Faussett Collection.**
8. On the true **Character of the Biographer Asser.**
9. Anglo-Saxon **Architecture,** illustrated from Illuminated Manuscripts.
10. On the Literary History of Geoffrey of Monmouth's **History of the Britons,** and of the Romantic Cycle of King Arthur.
11. **On Saints' Lives and Miracles.**
12. On Antiquarian Excavations and Researches in the Middle Ages.
13. On the Ancient Map of the World preserved in Hereford Cathedral, as illustrative of the History of Geography in the Middle Ages.
14. On the History of the English Language.
15. On the Abacus, or Mediæval System of Arithmetic.
16. On the Antiquity of Dates **expressed in Arabic Numerals.**
17. Remarks on an Ivory **Casket of the beginning of the Fourteenth Century.**
18. On the Carvings of the Stalls in Cathedral and Collegiate Churches.
19. Illustrations of some Questions relating to Architectural Antiquities— (*a*) Mediæval Architecture illustrated from Illuminated Manuscripts; (*b*) A Word on Mediæval Bridge Builders; (*c*) On the Remains of proscribed Races in Mediæval **and** Modern Society, as explaining certain peculiarities in Old Churches.
20. On the Origin of Rhymes in Mediæval Poetry, and its bearing on the Authenticity of the Early Welsh Poems.
21. On the History of the Drama in the Middle Ages.
22. On the Literature of the Troubadours.
23. On the History of Comic Literature during the Middle Ages.
24. On the Satirical Literature of the Reformation.

" Mr. Wright is a man who thinks for himself, and one who has evidently a title to do so. Some of the opinions published in these Essays are, he tells us, the result of his own observations or reflections, and are contrary to what have long been those of our own antiquaries and historians."—*Spectator.*

" Two volumes exceedingly valuable and important to all who are interested in the Archæology of the Middle Ages; no mere compilations, but replete with fine reasoning, new theories, and useful information, put in an intelligible manner on subjects that have been hitherto but imperfectly understood."—*London Review.*

JOHN RUSSELL SMITH, 36, SOHO SQUARE, LONDON.

ESSAYS ON THE LITERATURE, POPULAR SUPERSTITIONS, AND HISTORY OF ENGLAND IN THE MIDDLE AGES.

BY THOMAS WRIGHT, M.A. F.S.A.

Two **vols.** *post 8vo. elegantly printed, cloth,* 16s.

CONTENTS.

1. Anglo-Saxon Poetry.
2. Anglo-Norman Poetry.
3. Chansons de Geste, or Historical Romances of the Middle Ages.
4. Proverbs and Popular Sayings.
5. Anglo-Latin Poets of the Twelfth Century.
6. Abelard and the Scholastic Philosophy.
7. Dr. Grimm's German Mythology.
8. National Fairy Mythology of England.
9. Popular Superstitions of Modern Greece, and their connection with the English.
10. Friar Rush and the Frolicsome **Elves**.
11. Dunlop's History of Fiction.
12. History and Transmission of Popular **Stories**.
13. Poetry of History.
14. Adventures of Hereward the Saxon.
15. Story of Eustace the Monk.
16. History of Fulke Fitzwarine.
17. Popular Cycle, or Robin Hood Ballads.
18. Conquest of Ireland by the Anglo-Normans.
19. Old English Political Songs.
20. Dunbar, the Scottish Poet.

By the same Author.

SAINT PATRICK'S PURGATORY;

AN ESSAY ON THE LEGENDS OF HELL, PURGATORY, AND PARADISE, CURRENT DURING THE MIDDLE AGES.

Post 8vo. cloth, 6s.

"It must be observed that this is not a mere account of St. Patrick's Purgatory, but a complete history of the legends and superstitions relating to the subject, from the earliest times, rescued from old MSS. as well as from old printed books. Moreover, it embraces a singular chapter of literary history omitted by Warton and all former writers with whom we are acquainted; and we think we may add, that it forms the best introduction to Dante that has yet been published."—*Literary Gazette.*

"This appears to be a curious and even amusing book on the singular subject of Purgatory, in which the idle and fearful dreams of superstition are shown to be first narrated as tales, and then applied as means of deducing the moral character of the age in which they prevailed."—*Spectator.*

JOHN RUSSELL SMITH, 36, SOHO SQUARE, LONDON.

www.ingramcontent.com/pod-product-compliance
Lightning Source LLC
Chambersburg PA
CBHW032142160426
43197CB00008B/746